PRAISE FOR *MONEYMAKER* AND CHRIS MONEYMAKER

"An alarmingly seductive narrative."
—*New York Times Book Review*

"Razor-quick prose…"
—*Kirkus Reviews*

"I used to think my kid wanted to be the next A-Rod. Now all he talks about is Chris Moneymaker."
—John Saraceno, *USA Today*

"An overnight media sensation."
—*Washington Post*

"Another factor is poker's growing demand: A role model, former Tennessee accountant Chris Moneymaker."
—*Raleigh News & Observer*

MONEYMAKER

MONEYMAKER

HOW AN AMATEUR POKER
PLAYER TURNED **$40** INTO
$2.5 MILLION AT THE
WORLD SERIES OF POKER

CHRIS MONEYMAKER

with **DANIEL PAISNER**

Collins
An Imprint of HarperCollinsPublishers

HarperCollins books may be purchased for educational, business, or sales promotional use. For information please write: Special Markets Department, HarperCollins Publishers, 10 East 53rd Street, New York, NY 10022.

First Collins paperback edition published 2006

Designed by Daniel Lagin

Printed on acid-free paper

Library of Congress Cataloging-in-Publication Data

Moneymaker, Chris.
    Moneymaker : how an amateur poker player turned $40 into $2.5 million at the World Series of Poker / Chris Moneymaker with Daniel Paisner.
        p. cm.
    ISBN 0-06-076001-X
    1. World Series of Poker. 2. Poker. 3. Gambling. I. Paisner, Daniel. II. Title.

GV1254.M66 2005
796.41'2—dc22

2004054358

ISBN-10: 0-06-074675-0
ISBN-13: 978-0-06-074675-9

05 06 07 08 09 10 ❖/RRD 10 9 8 7 6 5 4 3 2 1

Sometimes nothing can be a real cool hand.
          —Paul Newman, in *Cool Hand Luke*

CONTENTS

MONEYMAKER

DAY ONE: MORNING ♥ ♣ ♠ ♦

I don't usually eat a big breakfast. Nine o'clock in the morning, most mornings, my stomach's not really awake yet, but this wasn't like most mornings. This was Monday morning, May 19, the first day of the 2003 World Series of Poker, and I was about to join 838 of the best poker players on the planet, on the floor of one of the most famous poker halls in the country, in a last-man-standing, knockout tournament to crown a world's champion.

I was here on a whim and a prayer and the fool notion that I stood even the slightest chance. I'd won a $40 promotional tournament staged by an online poker site called Poker Stars, and the first prize was a $10,000 World Series seat. I didn't win any money, mind you, just an all-expenses-paid trip to Vegas and the chance to sit across the table from these great players and get my ass kicked. Some prize.

The main event started at noon, and I couldn't see playing on an empty stomach. I'd be at it all day, with any luck, and I'd probably be too antsy to eat during the scheduled dinner break, so I ordered up a great, heaping plate of bacon and eggs and home fries. A glass of orange juice to wash it down. I waited on the food and tried to calm my nerves. The small restaurant was pretty much empty. A couple other guys—poker players, I was guessing—keeping mostly to themselves, getting their heads together for the first day. No one I recognized.

Not much in the way of a breakfast crowd around here. Not much of any kind of crowd, really, save for the players and poker groupies and friends and family. Binion's Horseshoe Hotel and Casino, for all its history and character, didn't really attract a typical Vegas clientele. The place was threadbare and throwback, more Holiday Inn than Mandalay Bay, more roughneck than highbrow. There was probably more denim and turquoise in this one casino than there was in the whole of Vegas—by the kind of wide margin some of these people would want to bet on. Folks came to Binion's to gamble, just, and they didn't much go for the pomp and glitz and sideshows the way they did at some of the shinier hotels and casinos. They didn't strut. They went about their business, and, for a lot of these people, gambling was their business. At Binion's—in the older part of the city, well off the Strip—the carpets were frayed, there were lightbulbs missing in the marquee, and the waitresses all looked a little older and a little more beaten down than they did at every other joint in town, but nobody cared. At Binion's the cards were all that mattered.

I was nervous as hell, and the time to kill wasn't helping. I'd never played in a live poker tournament in my life, and in just a couple hours, I'd be going up against the reigning legends of the game: Johnny Chan, Scotty Nguyen, T. J. Cloutier, Phil Hellmuth, Amarillo Slim. Their names alone scared the plain shit out of me, and as my mind raced over the list of entrants I'd seen registered for the tournament, I realized I wouldn't know half these guys if I tripped over them. I'd read about them. I'd heard about them. I knew Johnny Chan from Rounders, the all-time-greatest poker movie, with Matt Damon and Edward Norton and John Malkovich. I knew that T. J. Cloutier was supposedly the best player never to win the main event at the World Series. But I'd never seen them play—not all of them, not in any kind of studied way.

I looked around and tried to determine if any of these few other diners were checking me out, wondering who I was, whether I belonged. And I was wondering pretty much the same. Wondering, too, why I hadn't tanked the last couple hands in that Poker Stars tournament and copped the $8,000 runner-up prize, money I could have used with a new house and a new baby and enough credit-card debt to keep me up nights. Wondering if my Oakley Straightjacket shades made me look intimidating, or if the Poker Stars threads the company was making me wear marked me as easy pickings. Wondering how I might bluff my way through the first day of the tournament. That was my goal, going in, to make it through the first day. Wasn't much of a goal, but I was trying to be realistic.

I took my time with the bacon and eggs. Nursed that orange juice like I was on death row and this was my last meal. Knowing that, soon as I finished, I'd have to make my way downstairs to the poker tables and get myself killed. It was early, and most of the players in the tournament were probably still in bed, but I couldn't sleep. Tossed and turned and played out all kinds of imagined hands in my head. There was too much going on, too much to worry about, too much at stake. It was all just too, too damn much.

Slowly the restaurant began to fill, and by ten o'clock I needed to get out of there. I wanted to be off by myself somewhere, to stretch out some, get my head around what was about to happen, consider what passed for my strategy: to hold on, keep my cool, take some time with my cards. I told myself I'd wait a full five seconds before calling or checking or betting. Usually I make my moves as they occur to me, but I'd have to change my game plan to compete at this level, mix things up a little. Whatever the situation, it wouldn't do to be jumping into these pots on an impulse, without really thinking about it, not against the best of the best. Doesn't seem like much, five seconds, but it's all the time in the world when you've got a real hand. That was about all I had, in terms of strategy. That and the Oakley Straightjackets I was hoping to hide behind, not wanting to give away a thing.

I made my way down to the table where I'd be playing. There were ninety or so tables set up for the first day of play, most of them in a big room about the size of a football field. To look out on that room, with all those damn tables, was to grasp the magnitude of this event, begun thirty-four years earlier on a kind of lark and now one of the most popular world-class competitions in any sport—if you can even consider poker a sport. (Some folks do, I'm told, on the theory that if you break a sweat, it must be a physical activity.) Part of the appeal of the World Series was that it was open to anyone with $10,000 and the balls to go for it. "Anyone can win"—that's the tournament slogan used by the folks at Binion's, and it's a tremendous hook. Imagine being able to buy your way into the Indy 500 or the U.S. Open. To head into the same turns, the same dog-legs left, against all those awesome champions. It's one of the great thrills good money can buy, and these days there are all kinds of satellite tournaments and tie-in promotions that make it possible for amateurs like me to sit down at Binion's main event with a buy-in of just $40.

So yeah, anyone can win. In theory.

I was assigned to Table 8, which was in a smaller room of tables, downstairs from the main floor. Still a big room, but nothing like the football field overhead. There was no one around. It felt a little bit like I was at a wedding reception, and I'd wandered over to my table ahead of everyone else, and there was nothing to do but stand there awkwardly, waiting for someone to come join me. I set my Oakleys down on the table in front of my assigned seat—seat four—thinking my opponents would be by soon enough and see that I'd already been here, thinking maybe it would give me some kind of edge.

Then I rubbed the cloth for luck.

Then I left.

Headed back upstairs to the main floor, where there was a small gallery set up along the walls, rimming the tables. Just a couple rows of chairs and four or five rows of bleachers, and I climbed to the top row of one of the bleacher sections and sat down. It was about eleven-thirty, a half hour before the tournament was due to begin, and there was still hardly anyone around. Some security guards, some Binion's people, a handful of players starting to mill about their tables. Most everyone else was lined up at registration, checking in, running late. I lowered my head and set it between my hands and started massaging my temples, trying to block out the rest of the room, to focus, to get into some kind of zone. Shit, I didn't know what I was doing, but I had the butterflies like you wouldn't believe. I wanted the damn tournament to start. I wanted it to be over. I wanted to be in the middle of it, sitting behind a nice stack of chips.

I must have been a sight, perched there like that, legs propped on *the row beneath me, head between my knees, my hands rubbing at my scalp. Probably looked like I was winded, or nauseous, which I might as well have been. I don't know how long I was there—five minutes, ten— but at some point an older gentleman came over to me. I saw his shoes before I saw the rest of him, and I glanced up as he spoke.*

"First World Series?" he said, his voice easy with kindness and concern. He was chubby, with a wisp of mustache. He looked to be about my dad's age, and he seemed like a nice guy. He was big and (mostly) bald and six kinds of poised. He wore a loud Hawaiian shirt and a pair of shorts—a standard uniform for this event.

"First tournament," I said, sitting up straight, happy for the chance at small talk. I was dressed in khaki slacks and a black Poker Stars T-shirt, topped by my Poker Stars ball cap. Between the two of us, we could not have turned a single head.

"No kidding?" the man said, only a little incredulous.

I shook my head to indicate that I wasn't kidding. "How 'bout you?" I asked.

"Me?" he shrugged. "Oh, I'm out here every year."

"Really," I said, thinking I'd just met a tournament veteran, someone who could maybe teach me a thing or two before the cards began to fly. "And how do you usually do?"

"Oh, I don't play," he corrected. "I play poker, but I don't have ten thousand dollars to risk on a tournament. I just like to watch."

We talked for a bit as the room began to fill. Turned out the guy was well-known at Binion's for his crystals. Well-known all over Vegas. He'd go out in the desert and dig up these beautiful crystals, which some of the players would use as good-luck charms. They'd rest them on their pocket cards, or fiddle with them during the run of play, or spin them for something to do with their hands. He pulled out a crystal and handed it to me.

"Cool," I said, looking it over. And it was.

He told me the story of this particular crystal, told me where he'd found it—which part of Nevada—told me of its imperfections, its special powers. *"A crystal like this,"* he said, as if he were Yoda imparting ancient words of wisdom to some Jedi warrior, *"it will bring you strength and perseverance. It will bring you luck."*

"Cool," I said again, working the crystal with both hands, half hoping that, whatever special powers this thing had, some of them might rub off on me. Meanwhile I'm thinking, *Okay . . . what's up with this guy?* I'd never been one for mysticism or any of the New Age stuff he seemed to be getting at. I was glad for the company, glad for the distraction, but the guy struck me as a little bit off. Nice enough, but way into his crystals.

"How do you like your chances?" he said.

"I don't really know what I'm doing here," I said, being honest. *"I've only been playing a couple years. Online, mostly."*

"But you're lucky," he announced. *"I can sense you're lucky. Tell me, what's your name?"*

"Chris Moneymaker," I told him.

I'd been hearing cracks about my name my entire life—especially since I started gambling, and most especially since winning this World Series seat. I wasn't particularly up for hearing any more.

"With a name like that, you've got to be lucky," he said, sidestepping his chance to zing me on my name.

"I don't know," I said. *"I guess so, but maybe my luck is about to run out."*

"Tell you what," he said, reaching for the crystal and then holding it before me like a carrot. *"You make it to the final table, Chris Moneymaker, and this crystal is yours. I'll find you, and you can have it."*

"Thanks, man," I said. *"I really appreciate it."* And I did. Really. It was a great, calming thing, to have this slightly off, Hawaiian-shirted guy sit down beside me and start talking about the power of his crystals, about how he could sense my good fortune, about the strength I could draw from the positive energy all around. He lost me with some of what he was saying, but he grabbed me, too, if that makes any sense. It was almost surreal, and as I shook his hand, I wasn't sure I was ready for this strange, fleeting exchange to come to an end.

I moved from the bleachers and started to head downstairs to my *table, and as I walked away, I fought the impulse to turn back and ask this guy if he couldn't somehow loan me that crystal straight out of the gate. I mean, why the hell would he make me wait for it like that? Either he wanted to do me this solid, good turn or he didn't, right? Like I said, I wasn't much for New Age mysticism, but that final table was a long way away, and I needed all the edge I could get.*

1.
EASY MONEY

At the gambling table, there are no fathers and sons.

—Chinese proverb

First card game I ever played was bridge. Took to it pretty quick, to hear my grandmother tell the story. Said I had a real knack for it, and I guess I did, although, to tell the truth, I had a good feeling for any kind of card game. Whatever I was playing, I saw the cards better than most, read my opponents better than most, and knew what was coming better than most. I'll say this: me and cards, we got along.

Bridge was my grandmother's game, and she passed it on to me and my younger brother, Jeff, as soon as we could count and fan out our own cards. We were six or seven years old and struggling to hold and play our hands, but otherwise doing a good job of it with her seventy-year-old friends. Every weekend we'd drive to my grandparents' house on the other side of Knoxville, and before long my grandmother or my grandfather would bring out a deck of cards. I was usually my grandmother's partner, which I took as a high compliment, because in cards, as in most everything else, we Moneymakers liked to win. Hearts, spades, gin, cribbage—my grandmother taught me a whole bunch of card games, but we kept coming back to bridge. Everything else was what you played until you could get a good game going—and the good game was only as good as your partner.

My father's games were craps and blackjack, and I took to the latter soon enough, almost by osmosis. Craps was mostly a mystery to me as a kid, but blackjack made a kind of perfect sense; it seemed winnable, doable, even with the edge given the dealer. Dad played blackjack whenever he could—and talked about it sometimes when he couldn't—and I learned by watching and listening and later on by playing head-to-head with him in low-stakes or fun-stakes tutorial sessions. I learned the game in theory, and I learned it in practice, and here again it came easy. The nuances of betting would come over time, along with the ability to count and track cards without really counting and tracking cards, and the humility to realize that all this theory wouldn't mean squat at a real table, but I understood the odds and basic betting principles right out of the gate. That's how it was with most card games. Teach me a game and there was a good chance I'd get it in just a couple hands, and it was better than even money that I'd beat you at it before long. I don't set this out to brag—but hey, like I said, me and cards, we got along just fine.

Dad didn't have a regular neighborhood blackjack game or anything like that, but he found a whole bunch of ways to get himself out to Vegas or Atlantic City or some other casino—most times on someone else's dime. He ran the motor fleet at the University of Tennessee, but back as far as I can remember, he also ran a small travel agency as a sideline, and one of the great benefits to the travel business is the windfall of complimentary or agent-rate trips from cruise lines, resorts, and hotels looking to promote various packages. My father did a lot of cruise-line business, and I recall going on a lot of cruises during our school vacations. Every school break, or just about, we were off on another adventure. We went to Panama City often, and to Orlando, but the cruises stand out. We lived fairly modestly—my mother was a homemaker for most of my growing up, and we kids wore each other's hand-me-downs, and our house wasn't the biggest or fanciest by any stretch—but we took full advantage of these vacation deals, and some of my earliest memories were of my father, off in the ship's casino while my brother and I and soon enough our younger sister, Brandy, were skulking around the entrance, scheming our way inside. Security was usually tight on those cruise lines, and I don't think any of us ever made it onto the casino floor except to breeze by a slot machine and pull the handle on the fly, but that seemed to us the ultimate rite of passage. To be welcomed into those casinos, to drink and smoke and gamble—man, that was just the ultimate, and we held it out there as some far-off goal.

As vices go, my family had things pretty much covered, and in such a way that everything seemed to go hand in hand. My mother's family ran a liquor store—they still do, as a matter of fact, and we've all taken turns helping out at the store over the years—so I guess you don't have to look too hard to find the source of my lifelong hobbies and extracurricular activities. Kids are drawn to what they know, and, growing up in my household, I knew about cards and gambling and drinking. Taken together, these hobbies can be a dangerous mix, and there were times when I was stupidly determined to take them together and prove it, but each one on its own was mostly manageable, and I mostly managed to keep out of trouble.

For a good, long while anyway.

Outside of those weekend trips to my grandparents' house in Knoxville, and those frequent vacation perks courtesy of my dad's travel agency, our basement was the center of my universe. It was a real magnet for me and my brother and our ever-changing group of friends. It's where I learned to shoot pool and roll dice and play foosball, and to pit my skills against the other neighborhood kids'. I quickly realized that it wasn't enough to merely outshoot, outthink, outroll, or otherwise outplay my opponents. There had to be money involved—pennies at first, nickels and dimes soon after, and up and up. It was boring without a bet going. I couldn't see the point, and my friends seemed to hold to the same opinion, because we figured a way to build some action into almost anything.

At nine or ten years old, we'd invented our own game of dice. I guess craps was a little too complicated for us, or maybe it lacked the kind of head-to-head drama we seemed to crave, so we came up with a watered-down version. Three dice, one roller. The roller would bet on a specific number, one through six. If that number came up on one die, he'd get paid; if it came up on two, he'd get paid twice; if it came up on all three, he'd get three times his money; and, if it didn't come up at all, he didn't get paid. It wasn't all that sophisticated, but it was a decent game of chance, and it didn't take a genius to realize that, over time, the house tended to win. This was a small, dinky game of dice, and we were small, dinky kids, but even we could see how the odds tilted one way. And because it was my house, I made sure that those odds were tilted in my favor more often than not.

My buddy Troy Anderson and I were the ringleaders. I'm still close to Troy—he's the assistant chef at one of the restaurants where I work—and we're always reminding ourselves of the scams we used to pull when we were kids. Other kids collected baseball cards or played video games, but we hustled. Anyway, we tried. We were constantly inventing games and then trolling the neighborhood for our marks—a couple girls who lived on the street behind ours, four or five guys who lived on the other side of the neighborhood, some new kid just moved into town. Whatever crazy contests we'd come up with, we'd find some way to lay some action on it—and, inevitably, we'd find someone to take the bet. There was one game, a hockeylike contest involving shin guards and baseball bats and soccer balls that for a stretch of a couple weeks ran as a particular favorite, although I can no longer recall how we handled the wagering on this one, or if we even bothered. Mostly we bet on dice and cards and pool. Pool was my version of a sure thing. I was the best shooter in the neighborhood. Here again, I don't set this out to brag, but that's just how it was, and I played it to advantage. I don't think I knew the first thing about hustling, but I gave it my best shot all the same. And my best shot was pretty damn good. My grandfather taught me how to play when I was five or six—with little sticks, between hands of bridge—and I learned about spin and mustard and English when the other kids were busy learning how to read. I couldn't really hustle my friends, though—not because I had any great moral difficulty with taking money from them but because they knew they had no chance against me—so when it was just me and Troy or me and another good buddy, we'd come up with other contests to make things interesting. We'd hover over our bar-size pool table and come up with all these silly, convoluted ways to lag, and we'd bet on that; we'd bet on who could roll the cue ball against four rails and have it come to a stop closest to a mark we'd set out on the felt, and we'd keep at it until one of us was tapped out.

I was the best card player, too, only the cards didn't always fall your way, so pool seemed a better bet. I was also a kick-butt foosball player, but here again the ball didn't always roll the way you wanted it to, and every now and then even the best players can be beaten by a lucky opponent. I quickly realized that it paid to cut the odds in your favor in what ways you could. And so, more often than not, we played pool, where a strong player could essentially control the table. Ask any of my poker buddies and the folks I come up against online and they'll likely tell you I play poker the same way: I like to control the table, to set the tone, dictate the flow of the game. Otherwise, what the hell's the point?

I like to win, is what it comes down to, and I like to back that up with a little bit of money, and it goes to how I was when I was a kid. There was action in everything we did, even if it never really amounted to much. It kept things interesting, and it kept us on the edge of our little seats. On a good night, I'd pocket four or five dollars and I'd be on cloud nine. Then the next night, I'd give it all back. One night I took $80 off a kid from the neighborhood named Mike Cada, in dice and pool. I was twelve years old, and $80 was all the money in the world. Hell, I could get anything I wanted for $80, and I walked up the steps from my basement that night thinking life was pretty damn good. Eighty bucks! Naturally, I gave that money back over the course of the next week, but it was an impressive bankroll while it held out. That's how it worked with us, most of the time. We *traded* money more than we really gambled it. Or we took turns holding it for each other. We never really spent it on anything, just set it down in the pot until it was our turn to win it back again. Every so often, when we'd get a bump in our allowance or earn some small amount doing odd jobs, the stakes would get a little higher for the next while, but until we were teenagers, there was never much more on the line than bragging rights.

Gambling aside, our house was a real neighborhood hang. My brother and I were close enough in age that we had many of the same friends and many of the same interests, and when there were no other kids around, we had each other. There was always something happening. And my mom was always at home when we were kids (later on, she started working at her parents' liquor store), except I don't think she had any real idea what was going on downstairs. Oh, she definitely would not have approved of any gambling. No way. She'd have grounded us big time, and punished us a few ways more besides, so we were careful not to mention it. It wasn't like we were sneaking around behind her back or anything, but I don't think it would ever have occurred to her that her boys were shaking down their friends for their allowances and pocket change—because, generally speaking, me and Jeff tended to come out ahead. My father knew what was going on, and these days I'm guessing he was secretly proud, but he looked away from it. I imagine he thought it was healthy, a natural part of growing up, or maybe he just didn't think much about it either way. Maybe he thought it was harmless, which it mostly was. Remember, this was small-stakes, penny-ante stuff. No kid was ever down more than a couple bucks, and, with just a few exceptions, no kid was ever up more than ten or twenty. Every now and then, my dad would pull me and Jeff aside and remind us to be careful, not to bet over our heads. You know, standard Gamblers Anonymous advice, and we listened respectfully and then went about our business.

Trouble was, Dad was betting right alongside us, so I don't know that we could hear him through his actions. And it wasn't just an occasional run at the blackjack tables on our family vacations, or a Vegas junket every now and then. Each night, for the longest time, we'd go down to the basement to shoot pool. Me and my brother and my dad. My sister never really got involved, and my mom certainly never got involved. But every night there'd be some cash flying back and forth among the Moneymaker men. My brother was a very good shot, too, and we were supercompetitive. We always had a line of credit going with each other. Whoever was up one night would usually let the debt ride until the next night. Double or nothing—or some other way to win it back. It got to where I couldn't shoot a game of pool unless I was betting on it. It was no fun to me. It was just wasting time. I had to have some money on it to make it worth my while to even try. When I got older and started dating, I'd bring girls back to the house, and if we got around to shooting pool, I'd want to bet on it. I mean, how crazy was that?

I was also a competitive athlete, I should mention, and where sports were concerned, there was more than enough to keep my interest without my having to bet on things. I wrestled and played soccer throughout high school, and there was incentive enough in trying to beat the hell out of an opponent to keep the contests interesting. But wrestling and soccer were sports—physically demanding, punishing sports. Cards and pool and dice were something else. I was a sports fanatic. I watched baseball, football, and basketball. There was always a game on, and I was always hungry for some score or other, but I never knew you could bet on those games. Stuff like that just wasn't on my radar. I don't think I even knew what a bookie was until I was in college. My father never bet on sporting events—or, if he did, I never knew about it, and it wasn't until I went away to college that I put two and two together on this one and started betting on games. More on that in a moment.

My first significant losses came at the blackjack table, on a night that should have been mine. I had just turned eighteen, we were on a Royal Caribbean cruise ship, and for the first time, I was old enough to gamble. I was legit. My brother hated me as the trip loomed on our calendar, because he knew that I'd be the one finally allowed into the casino to sit with my father and gamble, and he'd still be left on the other side of the door. It was a great big deal, and I was pumped. I couldn't wait. I'd put together a stake of about $100, which I thought would be more than enough to see me through my first bumps of real action and onto a winning run.

I spent that first day on the ship chasing girls and catching rays and playing out every blackjack scenario in my head that I could think up. The first two activities were how Jeff and I had spent every damn cruise, but this worry over cards was a new twist to my routine, and after dinner my father and I went down to the casino as soon as it opened. He gave me another two hundred dollars, in honor of the occasion, and I thought that with such a huge stake, there'd be no stopping me. Really, I was thrilled. It felt like my whole life was about to start. But then a funny thing happened. Well, maybe "funny" is the wrong word, but it was definitely a thing. I couldn't catch a hand. I couldn't track all those cards. I couldn't keep myself from hitting when I knew I should stick or sticking when I knew I should hit. I couldn't concentrate for all the excitement. I'd played a ton of blackjack up to this point and thought through tons of eventualities, but I was still a green rookie, and I bet through $300 like it was nothing at all. Within a couple hours, I was broke. Busted. Done for the trip. It was infuriating, and heartbreaking, and I could have cried. Or shit. Three hundred dollars! As rich as I'd felt walking up those stairs with all of Mike Cada's money just a few years earlier, that's how poor I felt at this moment. Poor and miserable and pathetic.

My father took pity on me and threw me another $200, which I also lost in what seemed to me to be record time. I simply couldn't get a handle on the real deal. In all those teaching sessions with my dad, and in all those imaginary hands, I'd only played with single decks; with a single deck and only two or three players, it had been fairly easy to track the cards, but at a casino blackjack table, with six decks and a bunch of players, it was six times as hard. Hell, it was just about impossible, which I guess was precisely the point of all those extra decks. And to top it all off, I was nervous as could be. This was serious money, a fortune, and I was blowing through it like it didn't mean anything. I sat there with my fingers beneath the table, trying to count the cards as the dealer pealed them from the deck. For all I know, I was mumbling to myself, "One, two, one, two, one, two," as the hands played out. Up and down, as he continued to deal. But then someone would say something to me and I'd lose my place, or I'd stop to calculate a bet and I'd lose my focus. I froze. And choked.

And I swear, I could have choked on my losses. Really, it hurt to lose that much money that quickly—like I'd been kicked in the stomach. I couldn't bear to look at my father. Even worse, I couldn't bear to face my brother, who I knew would be waiting for me on the other side of the casino entrance, anxious for details. And worst of all, I couldn't face myself.

Five hundred dollars! Down the tubes! Just like that!

I guess that's why they call it gambling. I mean, if there really is such a thing as a sure bet, how the hell are you gonna find someone to take the other side of it? It was a real wake-up call, that first casino experience, and I wanted nothing more than to hit the snooze button and pretend it was all a bad dream. I wanted desperately to be back in our basement, where the stakes never grew too rich and the odds never grew too long against me. Where I had some degree of *hand,* like they used to say on *Seinfeld*—as in "upper hand." As I said, I like to have at least some control in a situation. I like to be the guy who runs the table, but here, out in the real world, I wasn't that guy at all. I was the guy who got his butt kicked, and I didn't like it. No, sir.

I'm happy to report that I recovered from that first humbling, humiliating casino experience—although I never recovered fully. That moment has stayed with me, and I'm guessing it always will, and I've decided that this is a good thing, a full-in-the-face reminder of how easy it can be to get sucked in at the casinos, how quickly you can move from hope to no hope, how all the preparation in the world can never fully prepare you for what you might face at a live table.

Back on dry land, I was once again too young to gamble legally, and that was just fine by me, because I liked the way things worked when I was gambling illegally. I liked the edge I gave myself in my basement—as the "house" in our dice games and as the hustler with home-field advantage on our pool table. I liked that I couldn't lose more than $10 or $20 before turning things around, and that even if I couldn't turn things around, I wouldn't miss the $10 or $20. I liked that I was back in control. A big part of the confidence I felt on my home turf was that I didn't depend on the money I made off the neighborhood kids in my basement. I looked on that money as a treat, a validation, more like a bonus than something I needed to fund my lifestyle. I actually had a bunch of minimum-wage-type jobs during my high-school years, and I looked to these meager paychecks to pay for dates and movies and video games and other teenage necessities; that was the money I counted on. I flipped burgers and worked the deep-fryer and the cash register at Krystal, a regional fast-food chain, and at Wendy's. I worked as a server at a restaurant called Calhoun's. I was like that guy in *Fast Times at Ridgemont High,* working every joint in town. And when I was a little bit older, I started working in my family's liquor store. I was one of those people who enjoyed punching the clock and going to work, so I never got to that place in my head where I figured the thirty or so bucks I could make on a shift didn't amount to all that much next to the thirty or so bucks I could make shooting dice or pool in my basement. I never made that connection. The hustling wasn't a source of income; it was something to do to keep things amusing, to add a little juice or action to our trivial pursuits. It was fun and games, nothing more. And a job was a job, something you had to do. The one could never replace or supplant the other.

As it happened, though, my job at the liquor store wound up enhancing or turbocharging these sideline pursuits. The drinking age in Tennessee was twenty-one when I was in high school, and yet there I was, even before I turned eighteen, with too-easy access to an endless supply of booze. If my parents' basement had been the neighborhood hang *before* I started working at my grandparents' liquor store, you can just imagine how things heated up once I went into the family business. It wasn't the best combination in the history of teenage diversions, but it wasn't the worst either. I was careful not to abuse that access, even as I took full advantage of it, if that makes any sense. (No, I suppose it doesn't make any sense, does it?) Anyway, allow me to state for the record that we never let things get too terribly out of hand; we simply topped off our fun with some underage drinking, and for the moment at least the drinking and gambling perfecta seemed to pay off. We all had a reasonably good time of it—all of us, that is, except for my father, who stepped downstairs one night to find a couple cases of empties littered about the place and me sitting on the couch sipping a beer like it was my birthright. Man, was he pissed! And rightly so. It was stupid and disrespectful of me to flout his authority like that, even though, to my credit, I was far less stupid and disrespectful to my parents than most other kids in my neighborhood were to theirs. (Not much of an argument in my own defense—but hey, it's all I've got.)

The *real* drinking and the *real* gambling didn't start until I went away to school at the University of Tennessee, where I might as well have majored in both. My other favorite subject was girls, and during the summer before my freshman year, I did some important preparatory work in this area also. One night my brother Jeff and I were driving around town with another buddy, not doing much of anything, when we happened to pull up alongside a group of three girls at a red light. Well, it doesn't take a lot more than the sight of three girls in a car at a red light to get three guys pulled up next to them thinking it's a formal introduction, so we rolled down our windows and tried to talk to them. I imagine we were something less than suave and sophisticated, but we somehow convinced this group of girls to pull over, and we hung out with them for a while until both sides felt it was time to move on. This was basically what passed for the dating scene among Knoxville high-school students at the time, and for all I know, that's still how it goes.

As usually happens, there was one girl among that group who stood out as the prettiest, and the funniest, and the coolest, and as we pulled away, we all started talking about her. Hands down, she was the class of the bunch. Her name was Kelly Weaver, and she had a sweet, genuine smile, and there was nothing to do but bet on her. That's just how things were in our crowd—we needed action on our action, and since we all wanted to go out with her, we figured we'd make it interesting. Five bucks to the first one of us to take her out on a date.

I was operating at some disadvantage here, because Kelly Weaver clearly hadn't been all that interested in me during our drive-by flirtation. Guess she sized me up and didn't much like what she saw. She seemed much more interested in my brother or my buddy and had likely written me off as an arrogant, full-of-himself jerk, which I had very likely been. Still, a bet was a bet, and a cool, good-looking girl was a cool, good-looking girl, so I was up for the challenge. I must have figured I could switch on the charm and turn things around, but I figured wrong. Turned out Kelly had a boyfriend, but what the hell did we know? I called her, and she blew me off. Jeff called her, and she blew him off. Our buddy called her, and she blew him off. And that might have been that, if we didn't run into her about a month or so later, walking out of a movie theater. Same group of three guys. Same group of three girls. Once again a too-familiar snapshot of the dating scene in our neighborhood, only difference being that by this time Kelly had broken up with her boyfriend. Course, we guys didn't know any such thing, and as we moved over to the girls to make inevitable, unavoidable small talk, I mumbled something intelligent to my brother, like, "Aw, I don't want to see that girl again, she's such a bitch." And why had I decided that this girl was a bitch? Because she refused to go out with me. Because she cost me an easy bet. Because she had a boyfriend. In all fairness, she was nice enough about it, but that still classified Kelly Weaver as a bitch in my book, and it entitled me to act like a drunken fool and generally make an ass of myself, which at eighteen ranked right up there with counting cards and shooting pool as things I was particularly good at.

And so, like an idiot, I *did* play the sloppy, drunken fool, and Kelly probably sensed that it was all an act, because we got to talking despite my lame approach. To this day I don't know *how* we got to talking, or *why* we got to talking, but we got to talking, and the more we talked, the more she didn't seem like a bitch at all. The boyfriend was history, and we proceeded to hit it off, and before our two groups parted, she suggested I give her a call. That first date would be mine after all. We walked off, and I thought, Hey, you never know, right?

Come to think of it, I never collected on that bet, but it's paid tremendous dividends just the same, because Kelly and I were married a few years later and ended up with one of the all-time-great how-we-met stories. We were a year apart—I was about to start classes at UT in the fall, and she had another year to go in high school—but we began dating, on again/off again at first, and things got pretty serious pretty quick, and when I finally got around to telling her she'd been the prize in our little bet, she took it in stride. Some girls would have been pissed to have been "objectified" in this way, but Kelly thought it was funny. Well, not at first, and not exactly funny, but she didn't really mind once we'd been together for a time. It kinda rolled off of her, which just goes to show the kind of good-natured, good-time girl she was. Hell, she'd have to be, to throw in with the likes of me.

I didn't know it yet, but I'd hit my first jackpot, and I went off to UT to claim the rest of my fortune. My first thought, before classes started, was that I would study to become a physical therapist or a doctor. Some type of career in sports medicine held great appeal—until I realized the enormous amount of work it would take to pursue a premed course of study. Me and cards, we got along just fine; me and schoolwork, not so much. The courses themselves were no problem; it was the studying that gave me some trouble. Specifically, it was the finding time to study that was the problem; there was too much else to do. See, I quickly discovered that studying got in the way of all the drinking and gambling and other merry-making I'd planned to pursue. As my first semester at school wore on, I became fairly skilled at picking easy enough classes and cutting just the right corners to where I still managed to pull decent grades. When my first transcript arrived, I was surprised at how well I'd done, considering how little work I'd put into it. Somehow I was able to make similar grades the second semester, and I think the lesson here is that if you're reasonably smart and able to figure out the drill, you can find the time to pursue all kinds of "extracurricular" activities.

The UT campus offered great and endless distraction. For someone who grew up bleeding Volunteer orange, I suddenly found myself with an outrageous front-row seat to the whole world of big-time college sports, and there was always a game. Football, basketball, baseball, soccer, wrestling—I'd watch it all, with a real rooting interest, and even though I wasn't playing, it still cut into my time in a major way. There was enough pregame talk and postgame chatter to get in the way of anything but last-minute studying. I crammed for exams and cranked out term papers the night before they were due, but I wasn't exactly the most motivated student on campus. I had other responsibilities. There was now the fair share of drinking I had to do, as a hardly responsible pledge at Pi Kappa Phi, and out-of-the-way card games I had to explore. A fellow pledge turned me on to an illegal, backroom blackjack operation in downtown Knoxville not long after I arrived on campus, and I checked it out with some trepidation. Remember, my first experience with organized gambling, on that Royal Caribbean cruise ship, hadn't gone particularly well, but I guess it hadn't gone badly enough to set me completely straight. I felt that I was due, that I had some balance sheet to settle, so I seized on the chance at this illegal game as a way to even out the stack.

This particular backroom operation was in some storefront basement, and there were two or three blackjack tables set up in a dimly lit and otherwise sparsely furnished room. It was all kinds of seedy and depressing if you looked too closely, so most folks tended not to look too closely. There were waitresses working the tables, serving drinks, but it wasn't the kind of place you went to for ambience. No, sir. You went for the cards and the action, and I took things a little slower this time around. I didn't do too badly either, actually made a couple bucks my first time there. I only brought $200 with me, which would have capped my losses somewhat if the cards went sour, but I went home with an extra hundred or so—and loose plans to return the following week. And I did. I made a habit of it, about once a week, and I was mostly ahead, until the cops shut the place down and I had to fish for another game. One would always turn up eventually. And there was usually a game at the fraternity house or in a friend's room on campus, but it wasn't the same as the real deal, so I scoped out these backroom games wherever I could find them.

My father's office at the UT motor pool was just a block or two from where I lived, so he rode me pretty good that first year. Banged on my door to get me out of bed in time for those eight o'clock classes that he knew I wouldn't make it to without an assist from my old man. It was good to have him around, even though he damn near drove me insane at times—just as I must have been driving him and my mother insane with my less-than-total focus on my schoolwork. Still, my grades were pretty decent that first year. I'd given up on the idea of taking premed courses, but I was doing better than okay with a general course of study. Plus, I'd fallen into a nice routine, pledged a great fraternity, made some terrific new friends, found a card game every here and there, and managed to forge something of a real relationship with Kelly.

And then a fraternity brother named Tony Schofield turned me on to a new kind of action that just about knocked me on my ass. It was a couple weeks into my sophomore year, and I was standing on the steps outside our frat house when the conversation turned to gambling. Tony let on that he had some money on the upcoming

Tennessee-Mississippi football game, and I was all kinds of interested so I pumped him with questions. I didn't have the first idea how to bet on a game, how to contact a bookie, how to consider the spread. I'd grown up hearing that so-and-so was a six-point favorite in this or that game, without ever fully knowing what that might have meant, and Tony very patiently explained to me how it worked. Tennessee was a heavy favorite, and I couldn't see betting against my Volunteers, so I asked Tony if he could place a $50 bet for me with his bookie. I no longer remember the spread, but I think I had to lay off ten or twelve points, which struck me as an awful lot of points to give up before the opening kickoff. Later on, I'd steer clear of those double-digit point spreads when my team was favored, but on this first pass, I didn't know any better.

Well, let me tell you, it's as if I'd died and gone to heaven. I'd always loved football, but it was like the thrill of a lifetime, watching the game with my fraternity brothers and having meaningful money on the outcome. Tennessee just destroyed Mississippi that afternoon—41–3 in Memphis—and despite the lopsided score, it was probably the most exciting game I'd seen to that point. It's like there was money riding on every play, and fifty good reasons to cheer. It was, I thought, the perfect marriage of my two favorite pastimes, gambling and sports, and it was about to take me on a wild ride that would end up costing me my shirt—and just about everything else besides.

DAY ONE: EARLY AFTERNOON ♥ ♣ ♠ ◆

I was still wishing on that damn crystal when I stepped to my assigned table a second time. It was about ten minutes before noon, and there were three or four other players standing behind their seats, looking their own kinds of nervous. Two of them—get this!—were also wearing Poker Stars shirts, and I took this as a great, good sign. I thought, Okay, Poker Stars players. I play with these guys all the time. I can beat these guys.

Then another player approached our table wearing a Paradise Poker T-shirt, advertising another online site, and an older gentleman stepped up wearing a green 888.com polo shirt, promoting still another online casino site, and I started to think maybe I wouldn't be so overmatched after all. It never occurred to me that these guys had any kind of sponsorship deals going with these sites, or even any ownership interests, just that they had won some other satellite tournament, same as me, just that the playing field might be a little more level than I had thought. I looked on at the billboards they were wearing and figured them for another bunch of amateurs.

A few of us made hasty introductions. One of the Poker Stars players turned out to be Jim Worth, who plays online under the handle Krazy Kanuck, and soon as he told me who he was, I about shit. I knew Krazy Kanuck. Everyone who played on Poker Stars knew Krazy Kanuck. He was one of the top players online, so I went from thinking I stood a chance against these Poker Stars guys to thinking they would have my number. Krazy Kanuck, anyway, would have my number. I didn't recognize the handle for the other Poker Stars player, and I took this to mean he was likely playing bigger limits than me, which couldn't be a good thing. Either he had money or he knew what he was doing, and on a handshake I put him on knowing what he was doing.

We wished each other luck, and I said something stupid and self-deprecating like, "I'll be in and out of here so fast you won't remember me." I wasn't posturing or roping these guys into thinking I was some patsy, but I didn't have a whole lot of confidence at that moment. It had been there, for a beat or two, but meeting Jim Worth took care of that.

Got some of that confidence back just a few beats later, though, when I shook hands with the Paradise Poker guy and got to talking. The two of us were the youngest guys at the table, by a bunch, and we compared notes. I told him about the $40 tournament I'd won to get here and assumed he'd won a similar tournament on Paradise Poker.

"Actually, no," he said. "I'm here because I won the two-millionth hand."

"Say again?" I said.

"The two-millionth hand," he repeated. "In the history of Paradise Poker. You know, ever. They had a whole big promotion, gave away this seat as the grand prize."

(For some reason I thought of that episode of The Brady Bunch where one of the kids is the one-millionth visitor to a movie-studio tour, and the whole family gets bit parts in a movie.)

"What kind of stakes you play?" I said, wanting to know if this guy was a player or just some dumb-luck mope who happened to be in the right place at the right time.

"Ten-cent, twenty-five-cent games," he said. "Just for fun."

Right then I was back in it. Here was a guy playing microstakes, just for fun, who happened to catch a round-numbered hand in the middle of a promotion. Here was a guy I could maybe pick on a little bit and play against. Here was a guy who might even have less experience than me.

We all took our seats, and I was liking my chances somewhat better—at least enough to hang around for the next while. I sat down in seat four. Jim Worth was sitting in the nine seat. The other Poker Stars player was in the one seat. The older gentleman in the 888 polo shirt was in the two seat, and my great new friend from Paradise Poker was in the eight seat. The other guys I didn't know but figured I'd do well to assume that they'd bought their way in for the full $10,000, that they were players—unlike those of us who'd won our way in on the back of a low-stakes online tournament. I took a final look around the table at all those even stacks of 10,000 in chips, because it's not often you get to see so many even piles of so many chips, and then I closed my eyes to the scene, wanting to put it on some kind of freeze frame, to where it would always be with me. Far as I knew, it might be the last time I was playing even with any of these guys, and I wanted to remember it.

First hand of the tournament, I was dealt an ace of diamonds and a four of hearts. I'd been thinking I should play my first hand, just to get my feet wet and chase some of these jitters, and a lot of the people I play against online would always play a pocket ace, but it really wasn't a strong hand, and I hated the idea of throwing away my first chips, so I folded. I wouldn't get very far in this tournament, playing nothing hands like this one, so there was no sense setting a bad precedent for myself. A lot of players called the big blind on this first hand, probably wanting to get a jump on the action, and the call ran all the way around to Jim Worth in the nine seat, who raised 150. No one called, and Krazy Kanuck had the first pot, and we were under way.

Took me a while, though, to get into the flow of things. I let the next couple hands go, posted my blinds when they came around to me, tried to steal a blind or two when I had position, and basically waited on some cards I could actually play. After the first few rounds, it became apparent that Jim Worth was raising my blinds every time out. Picking on me, the same way I'd planned to pick on the Paradise Poker guy—forcing me to pony up a whole bunch of chips just to stay in the hand. And there wasn't a damn thing I could do but to keep waiting on those cards.

Finally, a couple rounds in, I was dealt the king and queen of diamonds—the first hand I would actually play. I was in early position, and when the action came around to me, I counted out those five seconds I had pledged to wait and raised 150. We were on the 25/50 blind at this point, and this would go up every two hours, but 150 had been the standard raise at this particular table in this early going—three times the big blind—and since I hadn't really gotten mixed up in a hand yet, I didn't want to signal anything unbeatable. There was one caller. The flop came down queen-seven-five, which left me with a pair of queens. I made a bet. The other guy folded. And I won my first hand of the tournament.

Easy enough, I thought. Took a while, but there it was.

I was able to relax after that first pot, still taking a relatively patient approach. Turned out almost everyone at the table was playing with the same caution, except for Jim Worth, the Krazy Kanuck, who appeared to have it in for me. He raised another of my blinds just a few hands later. It was about an hour and a half into the match, and I was sitting with a six and seven of hearts, so I called. The flop was two-six-eight, which put me on a middle pair, which I thought was leading. I checked, and Jim bet 150—still sticking to the standard bet for our table, so it was tough to tell if he was sitting on a real hand or just going through the motions, busting my hump. I decided to come back over the top with 450. First real move of the tournament for me, and I felt pretty good about it. Jim stared me down some, and then he stared me down some more. I had my Oakley Straightjackets on, and my ball cap pulled low, determined not to give anything away.

After a good long while of this, the Krazy Kanuck threw down his cards. "I'm gonna let you have it this one time," he said.

"You need to quit bullying me, Jim," I said, hauling in my chips. I was trying to be good-natured about it, but there was probably some bite to my voice. He was just punishing my blinds, and I was getting tired of it. True, I was out to do the same to the Paradise Poker guy, but that was different. That was me picking on someone I had pegged to be a weaker player. I didn't like that someone had pegged me as a weaker player. It got my back up.

We bantered a bit, and I started to enjoy myself a little. I'd been so tense and coiled up inside when we started out that I hadn't given myself a chance to have a good time. But now I'd taken my first pot. Made my first move. Stolen some blinds here and there. I was up a bit in chips. Already we had heard that folks had been knocked out at some of the other tables, where the action must have been big-time aggressive, but we were all sitting pretty at table eight, sitting tight, waiting to move in when we had the cards, when the time was right.

Very next time I was on the blind, Jim raised me again—300, still standard for this table. We were now playing 50/100 blinds, so it was relatively early in the tournament, but I did not like where this was headed. When one guy keeps going after you like that, it's never a good thing. I looked at my cards: pocket kings. The odds of Jim sitting with the only stronger hand, pocket aces, were pretty slim, so I raised to 900. Everyone else had folded. Jim thought about it for a beat and called. I put him a lesser pair, or maybe an ace-queen, ace-jack.

As the dealer fanned the flop, I thought, No ace, no ace, no ace. Sure enough, there was no ace on the flop, and I immediately threw 2,000 into the pot. Didn't even think about it, just pushed in my chips and went for it. So much for my five-second rule.

Jim must have seen that I was a little too eager, and he folded, and as I hauled in my chips I could have kicked myself. It was a rookie mistake, to wait more than two hours for a hand like pocket kings and then to be so trigger-happy that you manage only a small pot—but I supposed if anyone was entitled to a rookie mistake, it was me.

Just a few hands later, I got a chance to make amends with a pair of pocket fives. The Paradise Poker guy was the only one who seemed to want to play, so I let him bet into me. I flopped a set of fives—two, five, queen—and I had to sit on my hands to keep from firing more money into the pot and checked instead. The Paradise guy bet 100, and I raised him to 300. He called. Instead of making a big bet on the turn, as before, I bet 500—enough to make him think about it, but not enough to scare him away. He called. I came back with another 500 bet on the river, and this time he folded.

I flipped over my two fives to show the Paradise guy and everyone else that I'd had him beat, and from that moment on, I started to get involved in more and more hands. Started to raise a little bit more. Started to play hands like king-jack, or king-ten, hands I wasn't touching just a couple hours earlier.

In general our table was tight and conservative. Everybody was folding to raises. No one was giving much play. Even our weakest players were still sitting with about 5,000 in chips a couple hours in, and our strongest players had built their stacks to only about 13,000 to 14,000. The player seated two to my left was turning out to be fairly strong, and at some point he started picking on me too, so now I had these two guys gunning for me. I slowed my game down a little bit and figured I'd ease off and let everybody beat each other up until I had a real hand to play. I went back and forth in my strategy, almost every round, but I was building a comfortable stake and developing some momentum and something of a personality at the table. That's how it is, when you play with a set group for any stretch of time; certain players emerge as personalities, as forces of one kind or another, and here I'd gone from playing fast and loose to patient and tight to fast and loose and back again. I was all over the place, and hoping none of these guys would know what to make of me.

About a half hour before our second break, three and a half hours into the tournament, our table was still intact. The older guy in the two seat wearing the green 888.com polo had been fairly quiet all afternoon, but he was starting to play a couple hands. And he was playing them well—well enough for me to get to wondering if he was someone I should be paying closer attention to. Really, by his actions and his demeanor, he seemed to be a formidable player, and I wondered how we'd gone all this time without my really noticing him. But here he was now, making himself noticed. He even started chatting things up a little bit, and one of the other players asked him a question about the 1995 World Series. Someone else called him Dan. He wasn't much for small talk, this guy, but he was beginning to relax and open up, and in the course of the conversation, I started to think, Wait a minute, I know who this is. This is someone I should know.

Next chance I got, I folded a nothing hand and stepped away from the table. There was a wall of photos next to the poker room, a Hall of Fame gallery of past World Series champions, displayed chronologically, and I moved discreetly toward those pictures and sought out the frame for 1995. And there he was: Dan Harrington. World Series Champion, *who also won the European Poker Championship that same year. Two gold bracelets. The guy in the green 888.com shirt. Two seats to my right all along, and I didn't have the first idea. I'd been so busy worrying about Krazy Kanuck and these other online players that I'd ignored one of the true poker legends.*

I was liking my chip position, and I was liking the way the tournament was going, but I looked back at Dan Harrington's picture and then over my shoulder toward the table I'd just abandoned and I thought, Jesus Christ, Moneymaker! You have got to be the biggest idiot in this room!

2.

NOT-SO-EASY MONEY

HOMER SIMPSON: Your mother has this crazy idea that gambling is wrong. Even though they say it's okay in the Bible.

LISA SIMPSON: Really? Where?

HOMER SIMPSON: Eh, somewhere in the back.

—*The Simpsons*

The gambling bug took such a big bite out of me at UT that it nearly sucked me dry. As with any addiction, it started in slow, manageable steps—which grew a little bit bigger and a little more unmanageable every step of the way. Over time these missteps took me to where I couldn't focus on much beyond point spreads and match-ups and tendencies. A big payoff was always within reach, and I was always reaching, and at the other end, it seemed my reach wasn't quite enough because I came up empty. Empty and scratching and dug in to some serious debt.

Here's how it started: My fraternity brothers were kind enough to turn me on to all kinds of new ways to bet my money, and I was kind enough to prove a sucker each time out, until I could bring myself up to speed. As I'd always been able to do, I caught on eventually and started winning some of that money back, but sometimes "eventually" was so long in coming that there was no way to scratch myself from the loss column. For one frustrating example, I never played much golf before I went to college, but a couple of my new Pi Kappa Phi pals were big into golf, so that's what we did. You'd have thought I was a lifelong duffer, for all the time I spent out on the links those first couple years at school—every day at times, when the weather was right, even if it was just for a hurried-up nine holes at dusk. We played *Caddyshack* rules, which basically means when you hit your ball into the rough, you get to put it on a nice little perch in the fairway and pretend nobody's looking; even allowing myself these generous lies, I was never better than a double-bogey golfer, and I usually left the course down thirty or forty bucks, but the thirty or forty bucks didn't mean that much to me after just a year or so on campus. It rolled off me.

It's funny, the way your perspective can change in such a short space of time, especially over such a key issue as money, and here mine would change about a dozen times more before my senior year at college. I went from feeling on top of the world with a wind-fall of $10 or $20 in my parents' basement to feeling as if dropping $30 or $40 to my fraternity brothers was no big deal—all in about no time flat—and from there things would change all over again, more and more and bigger and bigger each time out. It's like I kept adding zeroes to whatever numbers I could tolerate as losses and to whatever numbers I expected as winnings. The stakes kept getting richer and more meaningful, which in a strange way made those once meaningful pots seem hardly to matter.

Bruce Peery emerged as my main golfing buddy on campus. He was a tall drink of water who liked to gamble as much as I did, and we hit it off straightaway. He was smart and funny and didn't give a plain shit what was expected of him, provided he could claim a good time out of the deal and lay odds on its outcome. Before too long, he was my main drinking buddy, my main gambling buddy, and my main running buddy. Hell, we did everything together, or just about, and we still do. (Check out the edited highlights of the

2003 World Series of Poker, and you'll see him in the gallery, cheering me on alongside my dad.)

I look back over my various experiences at UT, and I'll be damned if Bruce isn't somewhere in the picture; if he's not front and center, he's off somewhere to the side, never too far from the action. The two of us took to sports betting in a big way, and early on, it seemed like it would stake us indefinitely. Bruce was a year behind me, a Pi Kappa Phi pledge to my veteran sophomore status, and he came along around the time I had my first taste of sports betting on that UT-Mississippi football game. He was relatively new to that kind of gambling, too, and we both fell into it at about the same rate, with the same kind of frenzy. We went from betting on UT games to betting on a whole slate of games, from fifty bucks a game to a hundred and two hundred, and so on. Here again, the stakes kept getting bigger, the action more varied, the outcomes more significant. Football, baseball, basketball, college and professional—everything was fair game, and we pretty much made a game out of everything. I looked up one day and realized I had a game going almost every night; there was always some kind of action somewhere, and by the time I stopped to catch my breath, I was up about $10,000. Ten thousand dollars! Talk about adding zeroes! I did the math in my head and thought, Man, it's just too easy! And it was! I studied the betting lines and the pregame analysis and followed my hunches all the way to some big-time dough. Bruce, too, was having a good run of things, right out of the gate. In the beginning we threw some money at one of those "pick" services—you know, those newsletters and tip sheets that tell you which games to bet and which games to avoid—and it seemed to work out pretty well, so we kept it up.

We fell into a routine. Most nights we'd sit around the frat house watching games on television. Usually we'd have three or four games going, and usually we'd have some money on all of them, if only to keep things interesting. There'd be beer and pizza and general merrymaking. It wasn't just me and Bruce betting on all these games; it was almost every guy in the house, usually in a friendly, head-to-head wager, although no one else had turned it into the kind of art form that we had managed. We'd start our days by waking from our stupors and Monday-morning quarterback. Early afternoons we'd kick around that night's lineup of games and see if there were any we liked enough to bet on. Late afternoons, we'd chase down our bookie and settle up from the night before, and place our bets for the night ahead. Evenings, we'd settle in for another round.

I was still working a couple shifts a week at Calhoun's, and for a spell in there I was running the family liquor store by myself, so there wasn't much time for classes and studying. I was too busy drinking and gambling my ass off to worry about such things— plus, I didn't really see the need. I mean, when you're nineteen or twenty years old and rolling in money the way Bruce and I were rolling in money, what was the point of classes and studying?

By my junior year, I was up about $40,000. That's an estimate, but it's a pretty conservative estimate—built on a reckless lifestyle that was anything but conservative. Not bad for a green amateur, eh? Bruce was probably up about $25,000 to $30,000. The two of us had more money than we knew what to do with—more money certainly than anyone else in our fraternity house, and more money certainly than we were entitled to, for all our sloth and ignorance and excess. Anyway, we were the money guys, and I'd lend it to anyone, for almost any reason. Lose to me on a bet and I wouldn't cut you any slack, but come to me for a handout and I'd cough it up. We bought all the pizza and beer. We subsidized all the parties. We helped guys fix their cars or otherwise save their asses, and we loved the way it made us feel. Well, I loved it. Can't speak for Bruce, although, looking back, he seemed to get the same charge out of the deal as I did.

Cards began to shuffle their way back into my life during the butt end of my college years, and I welcomed the chance to at least have a hand in the outcome of all this wagering. Sports betting was exhilarating and infectious, and for the moment it was paying off nicely, but I liked having a role in the action, and being in on the game. Bruce and I staged some spades tournaments with our surplus funds or stood as the house in some heavy-duty games of blackjack, but for the most part, these pots never amounted to much. Every here and there, we played some seven-card stud, acey-deucey, 727— whatever game the dealer could throw at us, we'd find a way to play it. Some of these games, like 727, weren't really poker games, but it felt to us like we were playing poker. We smoked the big cigars and talked the talk and fiddled with our chips, but some of these games fell short of the real deal. In 727, for example, everyone is dealt a single card, facedown, and the object is to land on the number 7 or the number 27. Face cards are half points, aces are ones or elevens, and everything else is at face value, and there's a round of betting each time new cards are dealt. The pot is split between the person who comes closest to 7 without going over and the person who comes closest to 27 without going over. All the subsequent cards are dealt faceup, so as the hand progresses, you begin to have some idea what each person is holding. It can be a complex game, and the pots can get up there pretty quick, but it's certainly not poker. Actually, it's more like a dice game played out with a deck of cards, but whatever you want to call it, we played the hell out of it.

Still, the cards were a sideline, something to do between sporting events. The real rush came in laying down big money on these big games, and yet for all this early, easy success with sports betting, I wasn't the sharpest tool in the shed. I knew what I was doing, but at the same time, I had no real idea. I was still subscribing to those "pick" services, long past the point where I could have done a better job of it myself, and still placing my bets with a campus bookie— bets that soon enough this guy wasn't able to cover. The holes in my game plan surfaced on a four-team parlay, an $800 bet that would have paid off at ten to one. A four-team parlay, for those of you new to this kind of wagering, is a turbocharged way to maximize the return on your investment; if all four games come in on your winners, you stand to clean up. And that's just what happened. I hit my four-team parlay and thought I was due another easy-money windfall, this one for $8,000. Trouble was, this guy didn't have the money to pay me, and I didn't have the first idea what to do about it. Really, it had never occurred to me that I'd get stiffed on a bet (by a bookie, no less!), even though in the real world, things like this happen all the time. Anyone can call himself a bookie, long as he's got the bankroll to cover his bets. I hassled the guy for days and days for my $8,000, with no results. I was pissed, but I wasn't about to go out and beat the crap out of this asshole, or any of that stuff you see in the movies. Best I could do was to bad-mouth him all over campus, and after a couple weeks of this, the guy folded his tent on his bookmaking business, which left me kicking myself for having placed such a large bet with such a small person.

That might have been the end of it, but I couldn't let it go. Eight thousand dollars is an awful lot to let go, don't you think? Well, it got to where I couldn't think of much else. I looked on at my gambling tab, which I kept in a notebook, and started to think of the money as a loss I would somehow have to make up. That's how it is, with winnings. Or at least that's how it was with me. I tended to earmark certain monies for certain expenditures or charge off certain losses against recent windfalls. Every entry was linked in some way to another, or to some real-world expense. If the Volunteers came up big for me in a basketball game, say, I'd look on the couple hundred bucks in winnings as a bankroll for a night on the town, and I'd enjoy that night on the town that much more knowing it was being paid for out of the pot instead of out of my own pocket. I guess you have to be something of a gambler to understand this mentality, but that's how it was.

Unfortunately, the inverse of this tendency left me looking for ways to make up this $8,000 "loss," even though I was still up a ridiculous amount of money overall. The best way to make it back, I determined, was to step things up a notch, to bet more aggressively, to load up on under-the-radar games with favorable spreads, and to do so in a way that protected me from deadbeat bookies. With these things in mind, we got a tip from someone about the offshore sports clubs that were becoming more and more popular at the time, and Bruce and I checked into it and figured if we opened accounts with one of these outfits, we wouldn't risk getting stiffed when one of our big bets came through. The money was virtually guaranteed, and the betting was virtually legal—and, I realize now, our downfall was virtually assured.

There were a couple of popular online outfits at the time, but we chose a club that took bets over the phone—wanting, I guess, to have at least some personal contact with the house. The deal was, you'd wire down some money Western Union, and when you were good to go, you could call in your bets and place them against your account, where your winnings would also be deposited automatically. I sent down $1,500 to get things started, and Bruce did the same, and the two of us proceeded to go off on another tear. I ran my account up to about $60,000 in the space of one football season. I mean, I was just killing the sports club—to the point where my father bought into my action. He couldn't believe the good run I was having, and he wanted in on it, so he anted up his share, and we went partners on the account. We'd make bets together, and we'd make them individually, and the way we worked it out was, we wouldn't have to check with each other if one of us wanted to make a last-minute play. He trusted me, and I trusted him, and for the first couple months, things were going full tilt. Really, I couldn't lose if I tried.

And then I tried a little too hard. (Okay, strike that: I tried *way* too hard.) I was attending a fraternity formal, at a fancy-ass resort in Georgia. It was a Saturday. We started in on our drinking early, ahead of the party. I threw $5,000 on Florida in the early-afternoon game, and the Gators came out flat and cost me some momentum, but in my win-it-back-at-all-costs strategy, this just meant I had to double up on the three-thirty afternoon games. So I laid $10,000 on Iowa and another $10,000 on some team I've conveniently erased from memory, and I somehow managed to lose both of these bets as well. By this point I was pretty steamed. Down $25,000, just like that. I still had about $35,000 in my account, and I might have just sucked it up and called it a day, but Tennessee was playing that night, and I felt certain the Volunteers would bail me out.

Realize, this was an account I was sharing with my father; we were in it together, and in it to win it, not to throw it all away. Realize, too, that the money involved here was *huge*—not just college-student huge, but real-world, high-stakes, lifestyle-changing huge. And realize, most significantly of all, that my father had no idea what my action was this afternoon. As far as he knew, we were sitting pretty with a roughly $60,000 profit and picking our spots, while in reality I was starting to drink myself off my gizzard, throwing good money after bad, and spiraling out of control—that's how desperate I was to recover from each loss right away. Bruce was essentially betting in step with me, so he was down a small fortune, too, and soon enough we were so hammered and so caught up in these bets we had no idea where our girlfriends were. We were getting updates on the scores through a service on our cell phones. We weren't even watching the damn games—which, after all, had been the whole point of this sports-betting nonsense in the first place.

So it fell to the Volunteers to make us whole, and I put $10,000 on the game and another $10,000 on the halftime score. That's always a bad sign, when you start betting on the halftime score—like you have nothing better to do with your money than to piss it away on a partial score that in so many ways has almost no relationship to the outcome of the game. But I was in too deep to see what I was doing. The only thing I could think about was clawing my way back to even, and all it would take was a dominant, wire-to-wire victory from my beloved Tennessee Volunteers.

The party was raging, and in every other respect we were having a great time, but underneath it all was this nagging, gnawing feeling that I was coming unglued. And I was. I was furious, and shit-faced, and gambling so far over my head and out of my mind that I should have been restrained. Bruce, too. The two of us were piling losses on top of losses—huge upon huge upon huge—and with each disappointment the stakes grew exponentially. I can't imagine what our poor dates were thinking. Hell, I can't imagine what *we* were thinking.

Turned out the Volunteers couldn't have covered the spread if they'd fallen on it, and at this point I was so far gone there was nothing to do but let the rest of the account ride on a West Coast game that meant nothing to me in terms of rooting interest and everything in terms of fiscal irresponsibility.

By the end of the night, I was broke. I was hit by that same wave of pathetic misery that found me on that Royal Caribbean cruise ship just a couple years earlier, when I'd blown my $500 stake at my first blackjack table in just a few hours. Here I'd blown through a whole lot more than that, which left me feeling a whole lot more pathetic and miserable. I was furious with myself, and dreading like hell the conversation with my father. How could I ever begin to explain to him what had happened if I couldn't even understand it myself? Really, I'd been so cool and methodical, building that account up to where it was. I'd thrived under the false impression that I could do no wrong, that the laws of statistics and probability somehow wouldn't apply to me, that I had somehow stepped in shit and stumbled across a surefire shortcut to ridiculous wealth and prosperity. And yet, even laboring under such sustained delusion, I was always careful to make good, considered bets, never laying too much on any one game and never letting my heart as a fan get in the way of my head as a gambler. To blow such a ridiculous bankroll on a couple drunken whims seemed so far out of character that I didn't recognize myself, but I didn't have to look much further than the bottom line on my account to see how thoroughly I'd messed up.

My father was incensed. Mad as hell. I'd never seen him that angry, even dating back to when he caught me defiantly drinking those beers in his basement. And I deserved every piece of his outrage. He couldn't even talk to me at first—that's how pissed he was at what I'd done—but more than that, I came to realize, he was deeply worried by my actions. So there was that, too. He was talking to me like a buddy done real dirt by another buddy, telling me how we would never gamble together again, how he could never trust me again, but underneath he was worried that I had a serious gambling problem. And I guess I did, only I was too close to it to see it at the time.

"You need to quit," he said to me one day, after the initial dust had cleared some. "You need to get some help on this."

"It's under control, Dad," I said, because I was telling myself that it was under control.

"It's not under control," he said. "How can it be under control when you get drunk and lose sixty thousand dollars? In one day? Sixty thousand dollars! And it's not even all your money!"

He had me here, but of course I couldn't admit that I had a gambling problem. I couldn't admit that I had done anything wrong or that I had mismanaged his money, any more than I could admit that I'd mismanaged my own. I had a score to settle, is how I looked at it, a serious debt to erase, and although I was still basically even on my college gambling career, I looked on this one-day hit as a $60,000 shortfall. I vowed to make it back. And soon.

Around about this time—surprise, surprise—my grades started to tank. I'd declared myself an accounting major, which struck me as all kinds of fitting and some kinds of ironic, considering the tabs I was tracking at the sports club and on my own notebook ledger, but there was no accounting for my work ethic. Hell, there was no time for a work ethic. My grade-point average went from 3.8 to .5 in the space of one semester, and in the spiral I went from having high hopes for a career to having no hope at all. How's that for a deadly combo? No hope and no bankroll? Man, I was reeling! The rest of my time at UT came to be about re-amassing that lost fortune, to getting back the money I'd lost. It wasn't about the grades or restoring my transcript to decent shape; it was about the money.

From that moment on, I never played any more than a couple hundred bucks on a single game. I caught some good runs alongside some bad runs, but I never again came close to that kind of money. I'd tasted it, and it was gone. When we were winning, things would be okay for a while, but when we started losing, it sometimes got to where we couldn't even make our rent. My parents had my tuition covered, and to a certain degree they helped with some of my living expenses as well, but if there was loose change lying around I'd lay it on some game.

At some point I thought it made good sense to start taking bets myself—I'm guessing this was on the confused theory that if I couldn't make a good go of it over the long haul on the sucker's side of every spread, I might as well stand as the house and at least turn some of the percentages in my favor. Kelly had started at UT the year after me, and our relationship was on again and off again, usually in sync with my gambling. When things were going well, I had the head for being in a relationship. When I was on a particularly bad run . . . well, not so much. Once, after a particularly good week, Kelly and I flew to Nassau on the spur of the moment and lived it up for a long weekend. It's like the money didn't mean anything to me, even though it clearly meant everything, and there I was just blowing it all on a trip.

We lived together for a time, but Kelly didn't have the stomach for these highs and lows. Who could blame her? She particularly hated the phone calls that would come in, all night sometimes, once I started taking bets, and these many years later, I'm surprised she stuck it out for as long as she did. Don't get me wrong, I'm glad that she did, and profoundly grateful, but I'll never understand it.

Really, I was a mess. My whole purpose in life was to get back what I'd lost, while all around me everyone was beginning to make big-picture plans. People were applying to graduate schools, getting good jobs, embarking on careers. Me, I was treading water. My grade-point average was crap. I went from genius to idiot overnight, and after spending four or five semesters on the dean's list, it looked like I wouldn't even have the grades for graduate school. Somehow I'd managed to land internships with some of the top accounting firms in the country—Arthur Andersen, KPMB, and Deloitte & Touche—but now it appeared I'd be graduating with something like a 2.8 GPA, well below the 3.0 I needed for most good graduate programs in accounting. I was pretty much screwed, but I kept at it. I still didn't go to classes with anything resembling regularity. I still took tests cold, if I took them at all. I still handed in my papers late, if I handed them in at all. And for the first time in my now checkered gambling career, I started to put some of my losses on layaway. All these years, and all this money changing hands, I'd always counted myself lucky that I was playing with house money, but sometime early in my senior year, the house money was gone and I still had the itch, so I started to charge some of these bets to my credit card, and before too terribly long, I'd built that debt up (or down!) to about $10,000. I drew a decent salary on these internships, but I put almost every paycheck to work on that weekend's slate of games, whatever the season. I'd bet on anything, I didn't care. I even started betting on horses at some point, which I should have taken as some sort of sign, because I didn't care the first thing about horse racing.

Somehow, despite my sagging senior-year grades, I managed to parlay my internship at Deloitte & Touche into a spot in UT's graduate accounting program, in Knoxville, where I would earn my master's. I made up a couple courses and nabbed a couple key letters of recommendation, pointed to my generally outstanding transcripts from my first five or six undergraduate semesters, and managed to talk my way in. The graduate program was a blessing and a curse, both, because it kept me and Kelly together in a kind of subsidized environment for another year or so, and it allowed me to keep up with my gambling virtually unchecked. It also allowed me to run my debt even higher. By the time I got out of graduate school, I was looking at about $15,000 in high-interest credit-card debt and another $25,000 worth of car loan on a styling new Infiniti G20, cherry red. Kelly and I would talk about getting married, and then we'd stack her legitimate student loans and her sensible car loan against my insane gambling debts and my dubious car loan, and it'd look like we had no chance, so we'd change the subject. Man, it was intimidating, and frightening, to look on at all that debt and wonder your way to the other side of it. Best-case scenario, I thought, was to land a good, entry-level job at one of the big accounting firms in Nashville and start socking away my paycheck, paying down those credit-card bills a bit each month. I'd have to quit gambling for good—a tricky proposition for a guy like me who always knew, back of my head, that another four-team parlay was just around the corner, that the next turn card could always be mine.

So what the hell did I do? I kept playing—a little more conservatively, perhaps, and a little less frequently, but I realized I needed something on the line, something to shoot for, as much as I needed that steady, socked-away paycheck. I needed the juice, was what it came down to. I landed a great job at Deloitte & Touche, in Nashville, and almost immediately I began scoping out some of the card games in town. It was a different kind of action from Knoxville, and with cards I allowed myself to feel like I was a bit more in control, like I was running the pool table again. A good number of my UT buddies had settled in Nashville, so there was always an informal game to be found, and there was no shortage of running buddies if I wanted to seek out one of the illegal card rooms in town. I'd play a couple times a week, and I didn't make much of a dent in my tab for the first while, but at the same time, I didn't lose any more money either. I counted this last as a good thing—and kept playing.

Bruce had a cousin, Dave Whitis, and he and I started hanging around a lot early on in my Nashville days, and playing a lot of poker. Dave introduced me to a buddy of his named Nathan Forest, and Nathan was really the first guy I met who'd played poker in the poker rooms out in Vegas and in the casinos in nearby Tunica, Mississippi, which was about a four-hour drive from Nashville. Most of the guys I'd been playing cards with didn't really travel in the casino crowd, so Nathan was a revelation, and one night he came back with a game called Texas Hold 'Em. None of us had ever heard of it, and he took us pretty good that first night. It's such a deceptively simple game that you come away from a practice hand thinking you have it down, but then when you start playing for real, all kinds of nuances and subtleties come into play. We all sucked at it, and Nathan took full advantage, but I had that pretty knack when it came to cards, and I knew if I kept at it, I'd have a shot to win back my share, and then some. I was the first one in our group outside of Nathan to get any kind of handle on the game, but I was still real stupid about it. Nathan, though, he kept pressing it. Every time he had the deal, he'd deal a hand of Hold 'Em, and eventually I got a little less stupid. It got to where I felt confident enough to seek out a card room where they only played Hold 'Em, and the first night I was there, I built up a stake of about $2,500. I still had no real idea what I was doing, but I thought I did, and that can sometimes be enough over a short stretch if the cards happen to fall your way; it can also get you into a stack of trouble if they don't. Next night I went to the same card room and gave the money right back, so obviously I still had a lot to learn.

The object of Texas Hold 'Em, currently the most popular game of poker being played in the country and the standard for almost every major world-class tournament, is to draw the strongest five-card poker hand from two pocket cards and five community cards. Or to die trying. It's probably the easiest poker game to understand, because you're really working with only two cards that are yours alone, and yet it's probably the most difficult to master, because there are so many different ways to play those two cards. The game rewards aggressive play, but it also rewards a passive style—especially in its "no limit" form. You can bet a lot, or you can fold a lot. You can be smart or crazy, conservative or reckless, patient or impulsive. There's no one proven method or strategy. It all depends on the table, and the cards, and a whole mess of other intangibles, which is why I think it's become so popular. Anyway, that's why I was drawn to it and why it quickly replaced sports gambling as my consuming passion.

Think about it: It doesn't take much beyond deep pockets and a serious set of stones to bet big money on a football game. And it doesn't take much to run a pool table, beyond skill and precision and hours and hours of practice. Blackjack is all about counting cards and playing the percentages, and craps is just a crapshoot. But poker? Texas Hold 'Em? Well, here you'll need smarts and guile and intuition and experience and balls. A beginner can get lucky and win in the short term. Anybody can win a couple hands running. But, over time, the player with the most smarts and guile and intuition and experience, and the biggest balls, is always going to win. Always. It won't matter what cards you've been dealt, it won't matter what position you're sitting in, and it won't matter that you're due for a good run. That's the beauty of the game. Until you learn how to read people, read a table, read your cards, you're going to be a dead player—as I was about to discover, firsthand.

DAY ONE: LATE AFTERNOON ♥ ♣ ♠ ♦

Before heading back to my table from that Hall of Fame picture gallery, I decided to seek out my dad. He'd flown in from Tennessee the night before to cheer me on, and I hadn't really had a chance to talk to him all day. Seen him to say hello, but that was about it.

I had to hand it to him, sitting through these early rounds, enthusiastic as hell and having himself a good old time even though he was back behind the rail where he couldn't actually see the action at my table. Really, it couldn't have been all that interesting. You have to realize, when they show these tournaments on television, the whole thing has been edited and highlighted, and there's all kinds of commentary and graphics and background information they keep throwing at you on top of the action. Plus, you get to see the hole cards, so you know where everyone stands. You see the odds and probabilities right there on the screen. Sometimes you even see the "out" cards a player needs to win the hand. Watching one of these tournaments live, though, you don't see any of that. You don't have any real idea what's going on, except for whatever body language you can pick up across the crowded room. You'll hear some whooping and hollering and have to figure out what it might mean. It's pretty much like watching paint dry, especially when the guy you're rooting for is thirty or forty yards away, but my dad was sticking it out. My buddy Bruce Peery, my other relentless supporter, didn't have that kind of patience. He was off somewhere at one of the side tables, working a game of his own, with other nontournament players, but my father didn't want to miss a thing.

I walked over to the bleachers where my dad was sitting and tapped him on the shoulder. He was surprised to see me in the gallery, and I guess when he put two and two together on what I was doing by his side, he must have thought for a minute I'd been knocked out of the tournament.

"You done?" he said, assuming I'd gone all in on a hand he had somehow missed.

"No, no, I'm still good," I said. "Up about four or five thousand. Holding my own."

"You should get back, then," he said.

I started to leave, but first I leaned in close. "You see that guy over there?" I whispered, pointing at my table. "Two seats over from me?"

"Green shirt?" my dad said. "All those eights on it?"

"That's him," I said. "That's a world champion right there. That's Dan Harrington." It was like telling him I was shagging flies with Sammy Sosa before heading back to the outfield grass to pick up my glove.

My father thought about this for a beat or two, and then he said, "Well, you just stay out of his way."

"Trust me," I said. "I intend to."

Once I put Dan Harrington on being Dan Harrington, I started to study his game. Thought back to how he had played so far. Watched him going forward. Thought how I'd handle him if we got mixed up in the same hand. Truth was, he didn't play too many hands, stayed out of the action a lot. Really, there wasn't much to go on. No one sat on his blinds the way they were sitting on mine, the way I was sitting on the guy from Paradise Poker, and it probably had something to do with the way the man carried himself at the table. Calm, self-assured, quiet. Like someone who knew exactly what he was doing, someone who'd done this all a thousand times before, someone you wouldn't want to mess with. That, or maybe everyone else at the table knew who he was and didn't want to tangle with a world champion. Maybe it was just me who figured him for an Internet player on a two-figure buy-in. I wondered what it must be like to be the kind of player where everyone else knows your style, your tendencies, where your poker history was common knowledge to everyone but a rookie like me. Where everyone is gunning for you, or afraid of you, or both.

In the middle of all this wondering, one of the tournament directors came by and told us we had to move our table. Took us all a little bit by surprise. There had been some movement at the other tables in the smaller poker room where we'd been playing, but no wholesale shifting of an entire table that any of us had seen. We were now about five hours in to the day's session, on the 100/200 blind, and more than a hundred players had already been eliminated from the field. Some big names, too. Our table was still intact, but there was so much reshuffling at some of the other tables that there was now room for the entire field on the main floor, so they kicked our group upstairs. Same seat positions. Same every-thing. We just bagged our chips and made the switch, and I couldn't shake noticing that there wasn't a whole lot of chitchat going on as we marched upstairs. There hadn't been much in the way of small talk all day long, and that wasn't about to change on this unusual shift.

Our new table was positioned right along the rail, which was great for my dad and my buddy Bruce when he checked back in, because now they'd be a little closer to my action. It was just ahead of the dinner break. We all looked at our watches and figured there was just enough time for another couple rounds, and I went back to studying Dan Har-rington. It was something to do while waiting on a pair of pocket cards I wanted to play. After a couple dozen hands, and immediately before the dinner break, I caught an ace, king in the hole, unsuited. Dan Harring-ton was the big blind, so he was already in on the action. I counted out my five seconds and raised into the pot—600, three times the big blind. Everybody folded around to Harrington, who called, so it was just me and him waiting on the flop. The dealer kicked out a queen, and two low cards.

Harrington checked.

I made another bet—another 600.

He raised me 600.

I called.

At the start of the hand, I was sitting with about 18,000 in chips.

Harrington had about 7,500 in chips. And here, after the flop, the pot stood at about 3,700. I had him about three to one in chips, but I couldn't put him on any kind of hand. He hadn't played all day long, not really, so I had no frame of reference for what he might be sitting on. Up until now he'd just made these tiny bets; most of the hands he played, he just checked and called. Best I could put him on was a queen pair, the highest pair on the board, or a high pocket pair of some kind. Hell, maybe he had pocket queens and that third queen on the flop had given him a sweet set. Or maybe he had nothing and figured he'd double up on his chips just before the break, give the rookie two seats to his left something to think about over dinner.

I was flying blind, but I was determined not to be outplayed. Not now, this deep into the first day. Not after I had built up such a strong chip position at my table. Not just before the dinner break. Not by Dan Harrington.

The turn came up on another low card. There was no straight out there. There was no flush. There was no obvious hand for me to put him on, but whatever he had, he was playing it. Big time. He bet another 3,000 into the pot, and this time I didn't need to count out those five seconds. They came and went pretty quick. I looked over at Harrington, to see if I could pick up anything from his demeanor. I looked back at my pocket cards, to see if maybe a queen had snuck in there to help me out. I thought, What the hell is he playing on? He had to have at least a queen, possibly a pocket pair. I couldn't think what to do.

At this point most everyone at our table had left for dinner—so it was just me and Dan Harrington and maybe a straggler or two waiting to see how I handled our table's first showdown with the world champion.

Seemed like I thought about my next move forever. I went over and over it in my head. Back and forth, over and over. I just couldn't put Harrington on any kind of hand, and the more I thought about it, the more I realized I couldn't afford to throw another 3,000 into a pot I had no assurance of winning. Not at this stage of the tournament. So I laid down. I pushed my pocket cards across the table and said, "All right, Dan. I'll give you the respect now. I believe you."

He reached for his chips and said, "It's good that you do."

He didn't show me his cards, and I didn't show him mine.

"Is it good for me or good for you?" I asked. I hadn't gotten anything from him during the run of play, and I guess I wanted to see if he'd reveal anything now that we were on a break. I figured, hey, it never hurts to try.

"Good for you," he said.

Okay, I thought. Good for me. I'd just blown 1,800 in chips on a nothing hand to a world champion who hadn't made an aggressive move in nearly six hours. But I'd saved myself another 3,000, and I was still sitting with over 16,000 in chips, still in a strong position going into the dinner break, still likely to last out the first day.

Trouble was, what was good for me was also good for Dan Harrington. As strong as I still was in my position, I'd also made him that much stronger in his.

3.

POKER STAR

Watch each card you play and play it slow,
Wait until your deal come 'round.
　　　　　—"Deal," The Grateful Dead,
　　　　　　　lyrics by Robert Hunter

I came of age as a poker player at about the same time live-action, online poker rooms burst on the scene, and it was a convenient setup. Don't misunderstand, online poker had been around for more than a decade by the time I started playing it in a big way in 2000 or so, in one form or another, but it wasn't until recently that these various gaming sites perfected the technology and provided a secure, controlled way to gamble in a virtual environment. Look back at the early days of online poker and it's not unlike comparing basic, first-generation video games like Pong and Breakout to today's elaborate video-game technology, but even through various growing pains the game had its appeal. Once the software was developed to where you could play in real time with players from all over the world and bankroll your action with a secure account, these online poker rooms became so popular there was sometimes a wait of several hours to get a seat at one of the higher-stakes, higher-profile tables—and on any given night or weekend afternoon, at any given prime-time hour, you might find fifty thousand players at active tables on one site alone.

I thought I knew a whole lot about the game, but in reality I didn't know the first thing, so I guess I chose to avoid reality wherever possible. I played online instead. A lot. At work sometimes, when I was on the telephone. On my lunch hour. At home, late at night. On some weekends I wouldn't even leave my computer. Mostly, while I was working for Deloitte & Touche and traveling the country doing audits, I filled the long hours on the road with a steady diet of online poker. After all, what the hell else is there to do when you're in the middle of nowhere with a nothing expense account and a bank account to match? I've got a picture of myself in my head, in an endless string of hotel rooms, sitting in my pajamas playing poker on my laptop in the middle of the night, convincing myself that sleep was a luxury I could do without. I was an information-technology auditor and it was my job to tool around the country to our various accounts and audit AS400, Windows NT, and UNIX systems. Online poker players all around the world became my constant travel companions. I played every night. It was a compulsion, and it was something to do, both. And I played almost every night when I was at home, too—and most weekends.

Eventually these countless hands played out online allowed me to gain some valuable experience in a fraction of the time it would have taken me in a flesh-and-blood poker setting, even as they left me a little less than sharp after an all-night session. I was feeling like an experienced, grizzled veteran with all the perspective of a green rookie, but there's no denying the sheer volume of hands I had played over a relatively short stretch.

I once put a stopwatch to it and figured you could probably play ten times as many hands in an online poker room as you could in a real poker room. That's huge. Think about it: Every time you play a live hand, the dealer has to rake in all the money. He's got to count out the chips. He's got to shuffle the cards. Players eyeball each other in search of tells and pause dramatically on their checks and bets and calls. There's small talk and all kinds of back-and-forth that slow down the action. Everything takes a little bit more time than it does online, where all the action is *boom, boom, boom.* Just click and it's done. Really, it takes about two hours in a card room to cover the same ground as you can in ten to twelve minutes online, and I very quickly got used to the fast, frenetic pace of the online game, the nonstop action, the constant juice. That's how I learned. A lot of players, I quickly realized, had hands going at three or four tables on the same site at the same time, I suppose on the confounding theory that even this fast-paced action wasn't quite fast enough, but I never had the head for more than one game. I liked to concentrate fully on the action at the table, to figure out the tendencies of the other players seated around me, to narrow the focus. Better to play one hand well than three hands miserably, right?

Naturally, virtual poker was no replacement for the real deal, and from time to time, I'd make a run out to Vegas to test my mettle in low-stakes games (twice, actually, and each time on someone else's dime), or to the just-opened casinos in nearby Tunica (every other month or so), and there were always out-of-the-way card rooms to be found in Nashville and Knoxville, but, to tell the truth, I preferred the anonymity of online poker. I didn't like screwing up in front of people who could see me—and, frankly, once I'd become accustomed to the pace of the Internet game, the live card-room action seemed painfully slow.

So I played online. A ton. Got pretty good at it, too. Got to where I had a feel for some of the high-flier players on the Poker Stars site where I usually played. Got to picking up tells from half a world away sometimes, based on how long certain players would take in responding to certain kinds of situations—although in the beginning what I mistook as tells could have just as easily been lousy Internet connections. Got to know what it takes to win, and what it takes to lose, and what it takes to pull a pot out of no hand at all.

I played small-stakes tables mostly—$1/$2, $2/$4 tables, sometimes $5/$10 tables. You don't lose a lot of money on that kind of game, but you're not going to make a lot of money either. As I got into it, I was playing thirty or forty hours per week. Poker quickly replaced sports betting as my vice of choice, and even though there was still money at risk, it was a lot more reasonable. I'd stake myself to $200, spend a couple weeks draining my account, and then replenish it with another $200. Nothing major. More of a slow burn than taking a torch to my money, the way I had been on some of those college football games. Before long I started to look on these inevitable losses as an entertainment expense rather than a gambling expense. Certainly, when set against some of those sports-betting losses I'd been taking the past couple years, it was a lot cheaper.

Money was a constant worry. I was making $40,000 at Deloitte & Touche, a decent salary for Nashville, especially for a young guy just out of graduate school—but it was never quite enough to make my particular ends meet. Things had been inching toward serious with Kelly, who still didn't have the full picture of my gambling activities. I was somewhat open and somewhat honest with her about my wheelings and dealings, but the out was in the "somewhat." I gave myself some wiggle room—which in turn gave me a measure of control over my out-of-controlness. Kelly didn't know how much money I'd blown in that offshore account, for example. She didn't know how much action I had riding on certain games. She knew when I was "up," and she knew when I was "down," but I don't think she was ever fully aware of the extent of my growing obsession with online poker. She knew and she didn't know—or, maybe, she didn't want to know.

As we got more and more serious, though, I came more and more clean, and once we started talking about marriage . . . well, then all bets were off—literally. (Well, *almost* literally.) We put our various debts together—hers legitimate, mine not so much—and couldn't see how we'd get out from under. College loans, car payments—that kind of stuff made perfect sense, and to update the figures I offered earlier, Kelly was now carrying about $20,000 in that kind of debt. Me, I was looking at a $50,000 hole when we got married, and most of my debt was gambling related. That wasn't good. Kelly—bless her!—knew what kind of creature she was throwing in with at this point and decided to marry me anyway, but she did not like the sports betting, especially when I was working through a bookie. She hated the seedy element I'd allowed to creep into our lives. She hated the way my losses would set us back. And she worried that these small-stakes poker games would lead me to bigger-stakes tables before too long. As much as anything else, she didn't like the way this gambling took up all my time. A full-time job, plus thirty to forty hours of poker per week, didn't leave much room for much else. Occasionally, when we were dating, I essentially ignored Kelly for weeks at a clip because I was so busy scratching, and we called it quits more than once over it. (For the record, it was Kelly who called it quits over the likes of me; I was too busy placing bets and playing cards to notice whether I was even in a relationship.)

The good news is that Kelly found enough to like about me to stick things out until I could see the light, and I think it was the winning combo of Kelly and poker that pushed me away from sports betting entirely. One of the great things about online poker is that you can have a game going and still spend time with your brand-new wife, as I quickly found out, especially if your brand-new wife is as patient and understanding as mine was turning out to be. She didn't mind if, say, we were watching a movie together on television and I'd be logged on to Poker Stars at the same time. She didn't mind because we were together, and because there wasn't a whole lot of money on the line, and because I wasn't much interested in most of the movies she wanted to watch on television anyway. She got the remote control, and I got the mouse and keyboard, and we called it a deal.

The whole lot of money on the line came into play when we decided to extend ourselves and build a really nice house we really couldn't afford, and to park our really nice cars in the driveway, and to treat ourselves to a couple really nice vacations we had no business taking. We weren't too savvy about taking on all these additional expenses, especially when we had that looming debt to pay down, but I guess we were young and in love and entitled to think that we would somehow manage. And we would have, too, if I could have managed to go cold turkey on the gambling. Kelly had a good job, pulling about half my salary, but with the car payments and the rent on our apartment until our house was ready and the building loan on the house and the general household expenses, there wasn't a whole lot left over after each pay period. We had a spending problem, which didn't exactly mesh with my gambling problem, but I wasn't prepared to give up the one for the other. I couldn't afford even the $1/$2 tables on Poker Stars, but I couldn't bring myself to give it up so I started playing the 25-cent tables. I also discovered these online tournaments that Poker Stars and other sites always run—some with buy-ins as affordable as $5, which entitled you to play as long as you managed to hold on to your chips, in a knockout, no-limit setting. In some of these tournaments, depending on the buy-in and the number of players, there was significant prize money to be won, so there was still some juice, some action, even though there wasn't a whole lot of my own money at risk.

For the longest time, I never even got close to winning one of those tournaments, I should mention, but I kept at it. In the beginning I played tournament, no-limit Hold 'Em like I would a ring game—a regular cash game. You can't do that, I eventually learned. The no-limit game is a completely different animal. I hated the idea of losing all my money in one hand. I sucked at it, and I went from being able to keep my account stable in cash games to making a little bit of a profit to blowing everything on these tournaments. Eventually I got the hang of it. I learned which hands to play and which hands to fold. I learned which players were reckless and unpredictable and which recognized at least some correlation between their cards and their betting. I figured out how to pick my spots and—as important—how to stay out of the way of other players who were off picking theirs.

I started taking notes. The Poker Stars site has a neat little feature that allows you to keep notes on opponents as you play out each hand—how much they bet when they're strong, how much they bet when they're weak, how often they tend to bluff and under what circumstances, that sort of thing. Or you could use the feature to keep a hand-history-type log of your playable hands. Most all of the online poker rooms have a similar feature, although there's no way to tell how many players take advantage of it; in my case I found it to be a tremendous tool to keep me focused on the competition. It's a good habit to get into—and I still keep it up. These days if I come across a player at a table with a screen handle I recognize, I'll do a search and see what I've written about him over the years. Even if I don't recognize the name, I'll do a search anyway, and, as often as not, I'll turn something up. Sometimes it's just a word or a note on a particular hand, and I'll call to mind enough to give me an edge.

The more experience I gained online, in tournaments and cash games, the better I was able to manage my online account. At one point I'd built the account up to where there was enough money to draw on it and to pay down some of our credit-card debt, so I was really feeling like I finally had a handle on my gambling. But then I'd head to Tunica with my buddy Bruce and blow $4,000 that I didn't really have—or money that we had earmarked for the house. Kelly knew what I was doing, and she never really tried to stop me, but she always sent me off with the pleading message, "Promise to leave us *something* in our bank account. Promise not to run us out." I'd give her my word—but I'd have tossed my word into the pot if it would have helped me to see a river card I thought I needed to make a hand.

Every time we'd climb out of our hole, by cutting corners and setting money aside to pay down our bills, I'd dig us a new one, and it's a wonder Kelly didn't run me out. We were in every kind of hole, in every which way, pretty much all the time, and it was all on my gambling.

(Man, I was a real good catch, wasn't I?)

In the middle of all this, Kelly and I decided to start a family. It was something we both wanted, but at the same time the thought terrified me. I thought, How the hell are we gonna afford a kid with all this debt on our heads? And the truth was, we couldn't afford a kid. No way. We couldn't afford the house we were building, the cars we were driving, the cards I was playing. Plain and simple. We talked about declaring bankruptcy, but it wasn't really an option for us. Kelly had her heart set on the house, and I couldn't see breaking it because of my gambling. We looked at all sorts of debt-consolidation services and started listening to this guy on the radio who helped folks put their financial houses in order. In the short term, underneath all this good advice, we decided to sell our two new cars, which would get us out from under a big chunk of that debt. We owed about $14,000 on Kelly's car and $24,000 on mine, so we sold out of those rides and traded them in for a $2,000 clunker Oldsmobile that used to be my grandfather's and a new $7,000 Hyundai that we bought for Kelly. (I'm sorry, but I just couldn't see Kelly and—one of these days—our new baby driving around town in a heap, and this was about the cheapest new car on the market.) The swap put us about $25,000 to the good and gave us a bit of breathing room.

I borrowed some money from my father during this period, and I hated like hell to have to ask him for it after what I had done with his share of our offshore sports-club account, but we had a great relationship, and he had put that $60,000 screwup behind us. I'd tried to make it up to him over the years; whenever I was flush with a good run, I'd throw him some money to pay off my stupidity, but we both knew I was making more of a gesture than a real dent in what I owed him on that score. And then, whenever those good runs ran out, I'd be back a couple months later asking to borrow $5,000, which he was always good enough to give.

Like millions of other folks, I lost my job in September 2001, in the sad aftermath of the attack on the World Trade Center. One

of our biggest clients, Service Merchandise, went bankrupt, and
Deloitte & Touche had to slash payroll. I was fired in the second
round of cuts. A lot of people were hurting—all over the country,
for all kinds of reasons—and Kelly and I were stuck. We were
caught between being excited about starting a family and fearful for
our future. The world suddenly seemed a messed-up, scary place,
and as I lay awake nights figuring what to do about it, I realized
that, in our own lives, I was responsible for most of the messing up.
It was me and my gambling that had set us back and left us scratching, and I vowed to do something about it. Unfortunately, what I
vowed to do was to get better at it—not at finding steady work,
mind you, but at playing poker. And I did, at just the right time. I'd
actually been considering taking on a second job before getting laid
off, as an outside comptroller for different companies, but there
were now whole chunks of my day where I had nothing to do but
look for full-time work and try to draw a semi living from my Poker
Stars account. I sat on my ass a whole lot and played a whole lot of
poker, and I actually did okay, for a while. Made enough to partly
support us—or at least to fill in some of the gaps of what I'd been
making.

Friends and family continued to help. Bruce was building houses
with his father and doing pretty well, and he very generously came
through with a sweet $7,000 loan to tide us over; my father anted up
another $3,000, although some of his investments had taken a major
hit in the stock market and he wasn't really in a position to be making such a loan. Some months later Bruce checked in with another
$5,000 loan, and we used this money to pay down our debt and pay
off Kelly's car and generally make things more manageable. We still
had to repay these monies to Bruce and my father, but these were
no-interest loans, and the terms were now much more favorable:
whenever-you-can instead of whenever-we-say.

I was out of real work for only a couple months when my old
boss at Deloitte & Touche arranged an interview for me with a local
restaurant company that was looking for a full-time comptroller. The

job paid $25,000—far less than I'd been making, but it was a good job, with decent prospects, and by the time I'd convinced them to give it to me, I'd talked them up to a starting salary of $32,000. Still not where I'd been, but I liked the people and I *loved* the restaurants. The company owned three popular restaurants in one complex downtown, including the Bound'ry, one of Nashville's best, and it would be my job to do the books for the whole operation. Payroll. Accounting. Receivables. Financing. Everything. Somehow I failed to mention to these good people that I hadn't been able to effectively manage the books in my own household accounts, but that was personal. I was skilled with numbers and other people's money—it was my own money I had some trouble holding on to.

Money was still tight, and there wasn't much left over for any kind of serious gambling, but I did keep my hand in several of these inexpensive online tournaments. In some cases it was cheaper than going out for pizza and a movie, and once Kelly and I found out we were expecting, in the summer of 2002, we started staying home a lot more, trying to get into good, responsible routines before the baby arrived—and trying to squirrel away as much cash as we could.

It was around this time that I started having some real success with these online poker tournaments, and I got into the habit of letting my meager winnings ride and using the money to buy in to whatever tournament I chose to play next. There was never enough in my Poker Stars account to make a difference in our lifestyles, but there was often enough to absorb an entry fee, and one rainy Saturday afternoon in April 2003, just a couple weeks after our beautiful daughter, Ashley, was born, I entered a $40 satellite tournament that, in success, offered a shot at a $10,000 seat at the World Series of Poker. I didn't think much of my chances, and I didn't have much use for the grand prize, but it was something to do while Kelly was busy with the baby.

There were eighteen people in the satellite draw—at two tables to start—and the deal was, the winner would be advanced into a bigger tournament to be held the following week, alongside other tournament winners and folks willing to buy in at a much higher level. I had the television going, and I was in and out of the room where the computer was—playing my hands when the house was quiet and sitting out if Kelly needed something or if anything else was going on. It was just a distraction, but the more I played, the more I realized I was kicking butt. I was drawing good cards, and I had a good read on the other players at my table. The quality of play in some of these low-buy-in tournaments is not always great. The better players frequently didn't bother. I don't know if this last was a factor here, but I ran through the field pretty quickly, and at the end of the day, I was the last man standing—which didn't entitle me to a dime in prize money, but it was the first time I'd won one of these things, so I didn't think to complain. What it did entitle me to was a seat at the next phase of the satellite tournament—a $600 buy-in tournament that would offer three seats at the World Series to the top three finishers and a fourth-place prize of $8,000.

I thought, Hey, this is kinda cool. I could never afford to risk $600 on such a tournament, and I had absolutely no use for that World Series seat, but I could have certainly used that $8,000. I marked the tournament on my calendar and decided to look forward to it. I'd earned my way in, so I might as well give it my best shot. At the very least, it would be the biggest tournament I'd ever played in, and there figured to be some strong players in the field. Plus, to bend a line from every golfer's repertoire, even the worst day at a poker table is better than a good day at the office.

As the week wore on, I built the tournament up in my head to where it was a great big deal. I asked Kelly if it would be okay with her if I checked out for the day, if she could handle Ashley on her own and leave me to the computer. She was fine with that and excited that I was excited, and on Saturday, April 26, 2003, at two o'clock in the afternoon, I sat down to play—with sixty-eight other entrants, all of them working their own version of the same angle.

Our computer was in a room in the middle of the house, and I shut the door and turned off the lights and pretended I was the only one home. I liked to play in the dark, because it was easier on my eyes over long stretches, and the darkness helped me to focus my attention on the action. It wasn't superquiet, but it was sort of quiet, and Kelly was good about leaving me alone to concentrate. Once in a while, when Ashley was asleep, she'd pop her head in the door and ask how I was doing, and I'd give her an update—but for the most part, it was just me and my online opponents. (Oh, and there was also Bruce, on the phone every now and then, offering note and comment on the action from his own home, where he was monitoring the tournament on his computer.)

It was a tough tournament to get a read on. In the beginning I was at a table where the run of play was a bit slower than I was used to online. Folks were taking their time with their cards. In the chat room that Poker Stars puts up on the screen below its simulated table, there was a lot of banter between hands, a lot of it focused on the upcoming main event at the World Series of Poker, to be held at the legendary Binion's Horseshoe Hotel and Casino in Las Vegas. Poker Stars was springing for round-trip airfare and accommodations as well for the three winners, and the mood of the chat room suggested that this was a coveted prize. Me, I still coveted fourth place. I thought $8,000 would go a helluva long way toward digging us out of our financial hole, while a seat at the World Series of Poker would likely get me nowhere past the first day of play. No sense coveting a souvenir-type memory when there was a good chunk of cash at stake.

Midway through the tournament, I caught an ace and tried to make some noise. I had 6,228 in chips, about average for our table—and, judging from the tote board I called up on the screen, about average for the entire tournament. We were on the 75/150 blind, with a 25-chip ante, and I was itching to shake things up, to tilt the action a little bit in my favor. I couldn't land a decent-size pot if I was guiding one in with landing gear, and we were at a point in the tournament where folks were getting antsy and moving all in on nothing hands. They were playing like they had nothing to lose, which can sometimes be a problem in these tournaments if you're not prepared to play the same way. I was in seat four, on the button, and figured this was as good a time as any to make some kind of move, and I got into a head-to-head battle with a player named GTHoldem, who raised 600.

I called.

The small blind and the big blind folded, leaving just me— Money800—and GTHoldem in the hand.

I held an ace of spades–ten of diamonds, and the flop came down four of diamonds–nine of diamonds–four of spades.

GTHoldem bet big into the pot—750.

I had nothing just yet, but I called.

We were each sitting with about the same number of chips at the start of the hand, so on a percentage basis, the pot was cutting seriously into our stacks, and I wanted to see what this guy was holding. If he was going to push me around on a nothing hand, I was going to make him at least show me his cards.

The king of diamonds came on the turn, giving me a flush draw.

GTHoldem bet 900.

I thought, What the hell does this guy have? The board wasn't showing much beyond diamonds, and based on some of the reckless moves this guy had made in previous hands, I decided to put him on a bluff. Then I decided I'd put myself on one, too, and pushed all in. It was my first bold move of the tournament, and I hated that I was doing it behind an ace-high run of nothing cards, but I felt I needed to be in a stronger chip position, to play more aggressively, to take control of the table. I also figured this guy had nothing.

And on top of all that, there was also this: Hey, what the hell . . .

So I sat there in our dark room, waiting for GTHoldem to throw in his cards—only half hoping that he wouldn't. A couple beats later, the icon above his seat indicated he had folded his hand, and I collected 2,900 in everyone else's chips, giving me the chip lead at our table by a wide margin. On a nothing hand. I decided to show my hand, which in an online game is a great way to posture to the other players—not because I wanted to rub GTHoldem's nose in my bluff but because I wanted everyone else to know that I wasn't afraid to go all in on a weak draw. It sent a powerful message—so powerful, in fact, that one of the other players, PK12, zapped me back a chat-room message telling me that he liked the way I had played the hand and that he was pulling for me to make it to the World Series to take down former World Champion Phil Hellmuth, the youngest guy ever to win the whole shooting match and one of the true legends on the tour, whom he seemed to have it in for. He started calling me "Get Phil," and even though I didn't have designs on the trip to Vegas, I'll admit here that I didn't mind this kind of attention.

A half hour later, on the 100/200 blind, I got involved in a series of back-to-back-to-back hands—five, in all—that were remarkable for the fact that they came one after the other and for the fact that they set me up nicely and loosened up my play for the balance of the tournament.

In the first hand, I was dealt pocket kings, called a 5,740-chip all-in bet, and lost on the river to an ace-high diamond flush.

Second hand I caught pocket sevens, was forced to go all-in by the very same player, and caught another seven on the flop for a full house, sevens full of queens, to win the hand.

Third hand the same player—Flerin—went all in again, only this time everyone steered clear.

Fourth hand, on the small blind, I turned over pocket twos in the hole, and Flerin immediately went all in against me.

That's four all-in moves in a row, from the same player, for those of you keeping score. My buddy Bruce certainly was. He called me on the phone after this bet and said, "What the hell's up with the Flerin guy?"

"Beats me," I said.

"Shit, I hope not," Bruce said.

I posted a message in the chat box: "Hmm."

Then I called the all-in bet from my weaker chip position—something I didn't want to do, but this Flerin person was playing so fast and loose with his/her chips that I couldn't let the move go unchallenged with a pocket pair. Flerin couldn't have pocket aces or ace-king every time out.

Flerin revealed five of hearts–three of hearts. A reasonable hand to bet, head-to-head, but nothing to justify an all-in move except for the chance to bully some of the shorter stacks at the table. Like mine.

Everyone else folded, and I typed in another message in the chat box: "Please, Poker Stars . . ." I did this on the theory that if the cards weren't coming my way, and if the chips were stacked too high in someone else's favor, it was okay to coax along some of each with an electronic prayer. And the side benefit was that everyone else would now know I could risk everything on pocket deuces.

The flop: ace of hearts, four of clubs, ace of clubs.

My twos were still good, but Flerin still had some outs. A three or a five would give him/her a pair to top my twos, and there was a nasty little straight draw that had me worried.

The turn: jack of spades.

Some of those same outs remained, but the cards were still with me.

Bruce had stayed hanging on the phone, so I said, "He won't be going all in like that so fast after this hand."

"Let's hope," Bruce said.

The river: ace of diamonds.

I took the pot with my full house, aces full of twos, and ran my chip count to 11,377, and on the very next hand I was pushed all in again, this time by a player with the handle ATL Angela—presumably a Georgia peach of some kind. I had a king-ten, suited.

She had an ace-ten, unsuited, and somehow managed to fill in a straight, ten to ace, on the draw, beating my pair of kings and knocking me back down a couple pegs on the leader board.

It killed me to lose a hand like that, but I reminded myself that this was poker, and that I was counting on winning a few the same hard way before the tournament was through.

In the space of just five minutes and six hands, I went from an 8,253-chip position to an 11,377-chip position, and then back down to 9,087. Flerin ran his/her chip count from 5,765 to 11,905, before sinking to 3,966 to close out the whirlwind. And another player, KillerAce, sat out most of the action and hardly moved at all over the same period, holding the table lead with 14,035 in chips, which just goes to show you that a flurry of activity is what you make of it. You can encourage it and throw your fortune to the cards, you can stand against it and hope your opponent is nothing but balls and bluster, or you can sit it out and leave it to the other mopes to knock each other off their games.

I set out this flurry of activity to illustrate how quickly fortunes can shift in an online tournament, with or without the benefit of cards. It has to do mostly with chip position and a willingness to bully some of the shorter stacks at the table—and a chickenshit, defensive mentality that seems to creep in during the middle stages of these tournaments.

I went all in again about forty-five minutes later, this time with pocket threes. I was kissing the chip lead at my table with 13,091 in chips. Two players—Messiah and Berkshire—each had just over 15,000 in chips, and both would feature in this hand. We were on the 200/400 blind, with a 50-chip ante, and Messiah opened with a raise to 1,600 chips. I called. Berkshire, on the big blind, also called.

There's never a lot of time, as the call whips around the table electronically, but there was time enough to think, Okay, this should be interesting.

The flop was three-jack-ten.

Berkshire checked.

Messiah bet 5,600.

I liked my set of threes a whole lot and raised 5,841 to push all in. If someone took the bet and hung on to make a better hand, I'd be done for the night.

Berkshire folded.

Messiah called, showing a pair of queens that would have had me beat before the flop.

The turn card was a ten, giving me a full house and leaving me to thank my chips for putting me in a position to get a little lucky on the draw.

The river was a king, giving me the hand.

It was, I thought, a key pot for me, because not only did I double up in chips, but I'd taken those chips from the table leaders—and in the time it took to double-click on the "Call" icon on my screen, I went from holding my own to holding everyone else's.

A couple hands later, a player named Eddieboy pushed all in. I led by almost six to one in chips at the start of the hand. I was dealt ace-king, unsuited, and I was happy to call with such a strong opening hand, especially from a much stronger chip position. Remember, it was Eddieboy risking all his chips on this all-in move, not me. The only thing I had to do was call his bet.

Eddieboy showed ace-six, suited, and I thought maybe he had someplace else he needed to be, which would explain going all in on an ace draw, suited or not.

The flop came four-queen-four, putting Eddieboy on a flush draw.

The turn was a three, off suit.

The river was a jack, off suit.

Our aces canceled each other out, and I took the pot with a pair of fours and my king kicker. Once again a little luck and a lot of chips beat the shit out of a little less luck and a whole lot less chips.

I'd been playing for over five hours, and I was liking my chances more and more with each hand. There were only about eighteen players left in the field, and as we approached the final table, I started thinking seriously about winning the whole damn thing. To be honest, I'd thought seriously about winning the whole damn thing before the start of play, but that had been pie-in-the-sky stuff. Here, now, I had a commanding position—better than a two-to-one lead in chips over the next-closest stack at my table, getting to where my opponents could no longer bet their hands with any real authority.

I caught a pair of pocket fours a short while later, still on the 200/400 blind, and my old friend KillerAce, who'd sat on his chips during that frantic all-in-o-rama with Flerin an hour earlier, was on the small blind, with 11,435 in chips, wanting to play.

I raised to 1,200.

KillerAce called.

The flop was ace-jack-jack, and KillerAce bet 800—a tiny bet from my strong chip position, so I called.

The turn card was a three, and KillerAce bet another 800. I couldn't understand the baby-step betting this deep into the tournament. Twice the big blind, with only five or six players to go before the final table. I put KillerAce on a bluff, which would have accounted for the tentative bets, and I quickly called. If KillerAce *had* a killer Ace in his/her pocket, it would have killed me in the hand, but these nothing wagers suggested otherwise. And even if I was wrong, I could certainly absorb the hit. It would have killed me in the hand, but it wouldn't have killed me in the tournament; hell, it wouldn't even have been a flesh wound.

The river card was a four, giving me a full house.

KillerAce bet 800.

I considered my options. With that four on the river, one ace in KillerAce's hole could no longer hurt me. I'd gone from being in an uncertain position before the river, where a lone ace could have put me out, to being far more confident. The odds that KillerAce was sitting on two aces were way big, especially considering how the hand had been played. The easy move, I thought, would be simply to call the bet, but I wanted to see if I could draw some more chips into the pot. KillerAce was down to 7,785 in chips—it said so right above his/her seat position. The other easy move would have been to push all in, which wouldn't have even cost me my table lead if I was wrong, but I worried that KillerAce wasn't ready to risk the balance of the tournament.

So I raised 7,600—giving KillerAce something to think about. Turned out to be a sweet little power play.

KillerAce called and turned over ace-queen.

It was one of the biggest hands in the tournament, and I wouldn't have won it if I hadn't caught that full house on the river—but I replay the hand here as a reminder that catching lucky cards is not just about luck. If my opponent had played the hand with any kind of authority, I would not have hung around to the river, and now that I had, it would be even tougher for my next opponent.

The bigger stack can always afford to get lucky, and this fact came into play just a couple hands later. We were down to only six players at our table. The blinds were up to 300/600, the ante still at 50. Berkshire, on the big blind, was my closest competition, with 15,267 in chips to my 46,732.

I was dealt ace of spades–jack of diamonds and raised to 1,800.

Berkshire called.

The flop was queen of hearts–ten of spades–ace of diamonds.

Berkshire checked.

I had a pair of aces and an inside-straight draw. I bet 2,400.

Berkshire called.

The turn card was the two of spades.

Berkshire checked.

The turn had been no help to me, and I figured it had been no help to Berkshire either, and my large stack enabled me to push my opponent around to find out. I bet 3,000.

Berkshire raised 8,017 to go all in.

It was a king-size pot, but I had to call.

Berkshire turned over jack of spades–ten of hearts.

My aces had the hand, and there'd be one less player to have to contend with, long as the river didn't turn up another ten.

The river: four of diamonds.

Eight minutes later there was my Money800 icon up on my screen, positioned around the final table with players named Big Orange, Hugefish, Bombardier, gotmilk, beginnerluck, shortstuff, JFGUAY, and First Ward. The tote above my seat showed me with better than a two-to-one chip lead over the next-biggest stack—57,007 to Bombardier's 25,860—and as we took turns knocking each other out of the tournament, the talk in the chat box turned to side deals. Remember, the tournament offered *three* $10,000 seats to the World Series of Poker, along with travel and expenses, and one fourth-place cash prize of $8,000, and when we got down to five or six players, there was a whole lot of out-in-the-open collusion going on. There was some private communication as well. I received a bunch of messages from other players at the table, wondering if I'd be interested in tanking a couple hands if I could still be guaranteed a top-three finish. You see a lot of this kind of endgame positioning in a knockout tournament—where, say, the last two players might agree to hedge their bets and split the first-place and runner-up prize money. I never liked the way these kinds of side deals cheapened the action, but here I didn't like them because I was still gunning for fourth place. I had a lot more chips than anyone else still left in the tournament, but in the back of my head, I was looking for ways to play my way down into that $8,000 cash prize. I didn't need to cut anybody else in on the deal; I could manage fourth place on my own.

I had all kinds of scenarios playing out in my head, of ways to creatively outplay my position, and when I bounced them off Bruce over the telephone, he tried to talk me out of it.

"Take the seat, man," he said.

"But I really need the money," I said. "Eight thousand bucks. What the hell do I need with a seat at the World Series?"

"It's not just the seat," Bruce said. "It's a thousand bucks in spending money, too. Eleven thousand, plus travel and stuff."

"I'd rather have the cash," I said. "We're strapped, Kelly and me. I owe you a bunch. I owe my dad a bunch. We've got the house and the baby. That's eight thousand dollars, man."

"It's the World Series," he said, like this was the only argument he needed.

"Yeah, but I've got all these bills," I said. "That eight thousand dollars is huge right now."

Bruce stayed on the phone for these last-gasp hands, and we kept going back and forth on this. Finally, when we were down to six players at the table, he said, "How 'bout if I buy half your seat for five thousand dollars?"

I wasn't sure I'd heard him right. I was in the middle of a killer 33,000-chip hand that I was still trying to win, but my pocket queens weren't holding up against gotmilk's pocket jacks with another jack on the board. "Say again?" I said to Bruce, after I'd lost the hand.

"Five thousand dollars," he repeated. "I'll give you five thousand dollars. Not another loan, but I'm buying half your seat. Whatever happens out at Binion's, we'll split."

I considered this for about a beat and half. I thought, Well, $5,000 isn't quite $8,000, but if you add it to the $1,000 in expenses, it's pretty damn close, and this way I'd still get to play in the main event at the World Series. Still get to have some fun out in Vegas, live it up a bit, see what happens. No way was I winning the whole thing. I was a recreational poker player. I was doing all right in this little tournament, but I wasn't any kind of World Series player, not by any stretch. So what the hell did I care if I sold half my seat to Bruce? I was like those guys in The Producers. First-place prize money was supposedly going to top $2 million for the first time in World Series history, but I would have sold half my seat a dozen times over, because 600 percent of nothing still comes up nothing.

"You're sure?" I said. "It's not like I'm winning the damn thing."

"They pay down to, like, fiftieth place," he said. "There's all kinds of prize money. You never know."

DAY ONE: EVENING ♥ ♣ ♠ ♦

Dinner break. First chance to really step away from the action, get some perspective on these early rounds of play. First chance to take a breath and put the game on pause. First chance, too, to get a good fix on how things were going at all these other tables. This last was key, because ours was probably one of the last tables still intact from the start of the tournament, and it was difficult to get the mood of the rest of the room in that type of insular setting. Strike difficult; it was pretty much impossible. No way to get any updates, from having new players sit down at our table bringing outside news or by joining a new table ourselves. No way to know what was really going on, to get any kind of handle. There was no leader board or big-screen simulcast or any form of big-picture bulletin on the tournament in general. Just a buzz every here and there, a small commotion when a table was broken up and players redistributed, an occasional sprinkle of applause as strong players were eliminated and ballsy all-in calls were rewarded. Enough to give us a sense of what was happening but no clear idea.

Binion's takes good care of its World Series players, but there's nothing excessive about it. No ridiculous ice sculptures or lavish spreads. Just a hearty, generic buffet set up in a roped-off section beside the lobby, free to players and available to guests for a small fee, so I gathered my father and my buddy Bruce and treated them to a meal. I was up about 6,000 in chips and feeling flush—even though, of course, I wasn't up any kind of real money at this point. I couldn't cash in my 16,000 in chips and call it a day, and I wouldn't see any runner-up prize money unless I survived to the third day of play, but I was feeling flush just the same. Hell, I was still hanging around, damn near the chip leader at my table, even after mucking that last hand with Dan Harrington. All was right with my world, way better than I could have expected, so why wouldn't I spring for dinner?

Didn't have much time, only an hour, so we sat right down, cafeteria style. Didn't have much of an appetite either, but I was hungry for talk of poker. I knew I needed to eat if I wanted to stay focused over the next couple rounds, but I didn't have the head for food. I wanted to hear about the action at the other tables. I wanted to know which big-name players had been knocked out and which had been playing well. I wanted to put the generally good run I was having into some kind of context, to go over certain hands, see if maybe I shouldn't have played them some other way. Bruce had been flitting about the room eyeballing some of the poker legends at the other tables, listening in to their small talk. And my father's a big, gregarious guy, and he'd been picking up a thing or two as well, so we compared notes.

Turned out nearly two hundred players had already been eliminated from the tournament by this point. I'd had no idea. Turned out, too, there were all kinds of players with much bigger stacks than mine. Guys were up 30-, 40-, 50,000 in chips, and I thought, How the hell are they up so big? I counted out chips in my head and thought there was no way I could ever catch up. The action at our table had been fairly tentative, conservative. Three times the big blind, pretty much all day long. More of a friendly game than a take-no-prisoners, no-limit game. There hadn't been much in the way of bluffing or posturing. No real pissing contests. If you didn't have a hand, you didn't play, only now I was hearing that things were ruthless and cutthroat and tense at almost every other table. Some guys were playing everything, betting everything, desperate for any piece of luck or edge, but that's not at all how things were at our table. Even our weakest player, the Paradise Poker guy, was still holding on with a couple thousand in chips, and I imagined that at any other table in the tournament, he'd have been toast.

Bruce had spent some time watching Johnny Chan and Scotty Nguyen and some of the other great players scattered about the main room, and it was as if he'd died and gone to heaven. Really, these guys were like poker gods to him, and to watch them from behind the rail, close enough to hear the clink of their plastic chips, to hear the confidence in their banter, was like having a courtside seat at a Lakers game during the finals. It was a goose, a thrill, and he told me what he could about their habits, their mannerisms, their possible tells. Course, I listened in and figured these guys didn't have any tells worth telling, other than the ones they wanted scouts like Bruce and rookies like me to mistake for an advantage, but it was information. It was something.

Best I could figure, our table was scheduled to remain intact after the dinner break, and so I spent some time going over my immediate competition. There'd be plenty of time to worry about Johnny Chan and Scotty Nguyen and everyone else if I managed to survive the rest of the day's play. For now the thing to do was to worry about the guys at hand. Jim Worth, the Krazy Kanuck, was running about even with me in chips. He was a solid player, who'd finally stopped picking on my blinds and had lately started to stay out of my way. I'd had a slight edge over Jim in chips before that last hand with Dan Harrington, but now there was only about 500 in chips separating us, and Dan Harrington had clawed his way back to even on the strength of my fold. The other Poker Stars player was also treading water at even. And there was another player, two seats to my left, sitting with about 13,000 in chips, but I wasn't too worried about him. He'd been aggressive at times, and for a couple rounds he had tried to push me around some, but over the past few hours, he'd seemed to set his sights on the Paradise Poker guy and some of the weaker players at our table. No sense beating up on the chip leader when the goal is to survive and there's an easier target within reach. That put five of us at about a push or better, and the other four at scrambling.

My father was headed back out to Tennessee sometime later that night, so we said good-bye at dinner, and I promised I would check in later with an update. He told me to keep doing what I was doing, not to let these guys intimidate me, to have some fun. I told him I'd try. Bruce told me to kick some butt, and I meant to make a good go of this, too. As we sat down for our fourth round of play, the blinds now up to 200/400, I could think of only one thing: Stay alive. Don't get mixed up in anything stupid. Survive the night and call it a day. A helluva day.

The plan was to stay out of everyone else's way, and I stuck to it. Stole some blinds, built up my stack a little bit, not really playing much. I don't think I showed my cards at all during the next hour, and I still managed to add another couple thousand chips. That's how it goes sometimes, when the blinds get bigger and you have position and everyone is stuck in defensive mode.

The Paradise Poker guy was the first player at our table to be sent packing. I wasn't involved in the hand that knocked him out, so I didn't pay attention to what he was playing, but what I did notice was the way he carried himself when his tournament was through. Like he'd seen it coming. Like it had been an honor and a thrill and that this was enough. He shook a few hands, wished everyone at the table good luck, told us he'd enjoyed playing with us, sounded like he meant it. He made all the right leave-taking moves, hit all the right notes, and as he went through these motions, I thought, Hey, that's how I'd like to play it when I get put out. Nothing melodramatic. Nothing hysterical. Just a genuine appreciation for a great good time, with no room for regrets or second thoughts. It was a welcome sight, because up until this point, every few minutes, there'd been some action, some corner of the room, some guy throwing up his hands or storming off in a huff or hollering some obscenity or other after losing his last hand, and here was this rookie, just like me, taking it in stride. Like it was inevitable. And it was. This guy was bound to lose all his chips sooner or later, and he'd managed to put it off until the fourth session, and there was nothing to do but shake hands and smile and be thankful for the shot. I thought, Okay, that'll be me. Not tonight, and hopefully not tomorrow, but that's how I'll play it when my time is up. Easy. Cool. Relaxed. Like I had it coming. Because back of my mind I was still thinking I didn't belong, still thinking I'd been lucky to be here at all, lucky to play this deep into the tournament, still thinking I'd come up against bigger and better and more aggressive competition before too long.

I reminded myself that my goal going in had been to survive this first day, and as we blew past the dinner break, I seemed a lock to last it out, long as I didn't screw things up. The thing is, there was another thought, somewhat further back, in that place in the way, way back of your mind where dreams go to die. Let's be honest—we all know that place, right? Where you allow yourself to think the unthinkable and then put it aside. I wouldn't have admitted it to anyone, and I worry that even setting it down here leaves me looking like I'm blowing smoke, but for the first time all tournament, another prospect had crept its way in to my thinking. And here it was: What if I managed to last out this first day, and the second day besides? What if, after that second day, the third day was there for the taking? What if this good run I was on didn't think to leave? What if I wasn't overmatched or over my head or overwhelmed, after all? I allowed myself to wonder these things, and in the wondering there was the faint whiff of hope that maybe I was meant to be here. Maybe I belonged. Maybe the way things were going at this first table would be the way things would go here on out, all the way to the final table.

Maybe.

Just maybe.

Shit, I thought. I'm not doing half bad. I'm hanging in. The chip leader at my table. Maybe I should stop thinking about lasting out this first day and start thinking about winning the whole damn thing.

And then I thought, Yeah, right.

4.

DO TELL

You can't lose what you don't put in the middle,
but you can't win much either.

—Matt Damon in *Rounders*

I called everyone I knew—at least everyone I knew who played poker, which cut the list down some.

It was late, around midnight, and most folks were out or asleep. Kelly had turned in much earlier, and I figured she'd be up with the baby in another couple hours and I could tell her the news then. But in the meantime I was bursting with it.

I called Nathan Forest, the guy who taught me how to play poker in the first place. He was happy for me, but he wasn't *too* happy for me. He's a big-time poker player, works as a dealer for a living, deals cards to guys like Scotty Nguyen at a casino in Tunica, and he didn't see any kind of justice in me sitting down at the World Series ahead of him. He saw himself as about twice the player and didn't see me standing half a chance. "Good luck, man," he said, not really meaning it. "It's like a billion to one against you doing a damn thing out there, but good luck."

I called my buddy Clint Marlar, one of the regulars in our local game, and he was genuinely excited. He's a med student at Vanderbilt, so it's not like poker is even a big part of his life, but he got what it meant—what it *could* mean, even. "Way to go, Money," he said.

I called Brian Lewis and Jay Pennington, the owners of the restaurants where I worked, and laid it out for them. "Can I get off work?" I wanted to know. "A week or so, next month, maybe two weeks if it goes well, out in Vegas?"

"This is big," Brian said when I explained to him about the tournament and the prize money.

"Go for it," Jay said. "Have fun. See what you can do."

I called my dad, and he was about as pumped as I was. Started making plans to join me at Binion's, for at least a part of it. Said he wasn't about to miss his own son playing in the World Series. Said it would be like watching me take a snap from center at the Super Bowl. Or something like that.

Man, this was huge. I'd watched the tournament the previous year, seen this guy Robert Varkonyi come out of nowhere to stun the field and take first place, so a part of me was thinking, Anything is possible. An amateur can take down all these pros. It's been done. Course, that was just a small part. The rest of me was thinking there was just no way, and I was along for the ride, nothing more. I mean, let's get real. I wasn't even the best player in our local game, hadn't even won a small-time Poker Stars tournament until just now, so I couldn't reasonably expect to make a strong showing among the best players on the planet. I'd only been playing, off and on, for about three years—and most of the "on" had been online.

Kelly thought I was putting one over on her when she woke up with Ashley a few hours later. Maybe it's because she was groggy and sleep-deprived, or maybe it's because stuff like this didn't usually happen to folks like us, but it took a couple beats for her to get her head around what I was telling her—and when she finally did she was all over it. Happy to send me off to Vegas for a week, long as it wasn't costing us any money. Happy, too, that I'd thought to cut Bruce Peery in on my action, which we both knew would go a long way toward easing some of our credit-card debt. Happy that I finally seemed to be taking some responsibility with my gambling—an oxymoron that even this moron could recognize was just a sugarcoating.

Anyway, last we talked, before she'd turned in earlier that evening, I was still gunning for that fourth-place prize money, so this was a serious shift in gears, me grabbing one of the grand prizes, but once Kelly was caught up in it, she had people she wanted to call as well. There was a part of Kelly that loved the action, same as me, which I guess is how she managed to put up with me, and here she was deep into it, same as me. Running the long odds against and still liking my chances, same as me. We were both over-the-top excited, and bursting with it, and anxious to see what happened next.

The next few days couldn't pass quick enough. Bruce and I hatched a plan to head out four or five days early, get some live poker-room experience so I could at least make a respectable effort when the tournament itself got under way. Spent some time thinking about a strategy. Considered what I'd wear, what I'd eat, even down to whether I'd drink soda or water or juice at the table. Nothing seemed too small a detail to worry about, because the bigger details—like, say, actually playing poker and knowing what the hell I was doing—were pretty much out of my hands. Got a jump on things at work, too, so the job would be covered while I was out of town. Covered every damn base I could think to cover.

And then there was a glitch. (There's always a glitch, right?) About a week before we were due to leave, Bruce came by and said there was something he needed to tell me. He had a kind of hangdog, weary expression that told me straight off something was up. I thought maybe he had to back out of the trip all of a sudden, maybe something had come up with him and work and he was bummed about it. All along he'd been planning to come and make a road trip out of it. My adventure was his adventure, and I don't know that I would have been up for it in the same big way if Bruce wasn't fixing to be at my side.

"It's the five grand, man," he said. "I can't do it."

This was about the last thing I was expecting to hear. It had just been a couple days, but I'd been counting on that money. Started to pay off some bills, even. "What do you mean, you can't do it?" I said.

"I mean I don't have the money," he said. "I wish I did, but I don't."

He was all torn up about it—and once I processed what he was telling me, so was I. Torn up and pissed and wishing I had those last few Poker Stars hands back to play all over again. I didn't hold anything against Bruce, mind you. He'd been a great and true friend. He'd bailed me out a whole bunch of times, and he'd bail me out a whole bunch more if he could. He wanted to bail me out here. It wasn't his fault things were tight. It wasn't anybody's fault, except maybe mine, and I kicked myself for not taking that fourth-place prize money when it was within reach. Kelly and I desperately needed that money. We needed the full $8,000, and I'd talked myself down to Bruce's $5,000 and the $1,000 in spending money, and now with Bruce out of the deal, there was just the spending money, and it wasn't near enough to get us even close to whole. I didn't have the first idea what to tell Kelly, and I put it off for a bit until I had a clue.

I told my dad straight off. He'd known the full story—the fourth-place prize money, the deal making as the tournament wound down, Bruce's offer for half my seat—and I guess I just wanted to vent. He'd known that Bruce had been there for me before and that he would be there for me again, and this was just how things had shaken out this time. Money was tight all around. I knew that things were tight for my dad as well, and I wasn't going to him for the money. I was going for advice, more than anything else, for some perspective. I guess I wanted someone to remind me that I was essentially in the same place I'd been before the Poker Stars tournament. That it was a disappointment, having to keep carrying all that credit-card debt, but it wasn't devastating. It was, like it or not, business as usual and more of the same.

But instead of talking sense, my father surprised the shit out of me and dug deep. "I can come up with two thousand," he said, "if that helps." He didn't have the money, and I didn't want to take it, but he insisted. It wasn't a loan, he said, but an investment. He expected 20 percent of my action, using the same formula I'd had working with Bruce, which had been based on Binion's buy-in price tag of $10,000 for a World Series seat. And he expected a return on his investment. "You can play with these guys, Chris," he said, "long as you think you can play with these guys."

Next I told the story to a friend of mine named Dave Gamble—how's that for another fitting name?—who also wanted to back me $2,000 on the same terms, and Clint and a friend of his named Mike kicked in $500 between them for a 5 percent taste, and by the time I told Kelly about Bruce, I'd managed to nearly match his stake—so it was a big deal and not a big deal, both.

Keep in mind, Bruce was still planning to make the trip with me. He'd already purchased his plane ticket, when he was flush, and he was planning to crash in the hotel room Poker Stars was comping me at Binion's, so his expenses were mostly covered. It was the money to burn he couldn't come up with. He came up to my office the day before we were due to leave and threw a bag down on my desk, said he'd bought me a good-luck present. I guess he was feeling bad about the $5,000—check that, I *know* he was feeling bad about it—and he wanted to let me know he'd meant well.

"What's in the bag?" I said.

"Open it," he said.

Inside was a pair of styling Oakley Straightjacket shades—a $100 pair of sunglasses, which was probably about ten times what I'd ever paid for sunglasses. They were killer. Cool lenses that wrapped pretty much all the way around to the ears. Like I said, styling. "These are expensive," I said.

"If you don't want them, I'll take them," he said.

"No, I'll take them," I said, and I tried them on. They covered my eyes real well, like a shield. Made me look menacing, like I had something to hide.

Bruce checked me out. "Cool," he said.

We'd talked about sunglasses, about covering up as much as possible before sitting down to my first table. (Shit, I would have pulled a jacket over my head if I could have gotten away with it.) Actually, it was Bruce's idea. "You need to hide your eyes," he told me one night when we were talking strategy. "And you need to stop looking away from people when you're bluffing."

"I don't look away from people when I'm bluffing," I said—most likely looking away as I said it.

"Money," he said, "I play poker with you. It's like to cost me next time we sit down at the same table, but you need to hide your eyes, and you need to stop looking away when you're bluffing."

I took him at his word and promised myself I'd work on it. There was a lot I needed to work on, Bruce and I were quickly realizing. For all the hands I'd managed to hurry up and play online, for all the insight I'd gained reading players I couldn't see, for all my instincts putting opponents on cards they couldn't help but have in a full-table, low-stakes online game, I had absolutely no tournament experience. I was so far out of my element it was almost funny. Tournament play—especially in no-limit's knockout format—was about as far removed from the $1/$2 tables on Poker Stars as chess is to checkers. The more we talked about it, the more I realized how essential it was to get my feet wet before the tournament started, and the $4,500 began to look like my seed money. Remember, this was money Kelly and I desperately needed to pay down our credit cards, but with the tournament approaching, I set it out there and let it play with my head a little bit. I told myself I could shave off $1,000 and stake myself to some live-action tables at Binion's after Bruce and I arrived. That would leave me with $3,500, which would still take a serious bite out of our bills. Then the $1,000 became $2,000—because, really, what the hell was the difference?—and then the $2,000 became $3,000, and so on, until I was thinking of the $4,500 from my dad and Dave and Clint and Mike as my nut and hoping like hell to parlay $4,500 worth of last-minute experience into at least some sort of payday in the tournament, else I'd be looking at the same stack of bills when I got home. I went from responsible to reckless to flat-out stupid in the time it took for me to kiss Kelly and Ashley good-bye and head out to the airport.

Poker Stars had a limo waiting for us at the airport in Vegas, and Bruce and I climbed in feeling like high rollers—which of course didn't help. Soon as we breezed into Binion's and set down our bags in our nothing-special twelfth-floor room where the air conditioner didn't work and the shrink wraps on the plastic cups in the bathroom had some big-time holes in them, we raced back down to the casino like the money was setting my pockets on fire.

First thing I did, world-class sucker that I am, was step into the sports club and lay $400 on an Atlanta Braves game. Greg Maddux was pitching, and it seemed to me a sure thing, and this was Vegas, and Bruce and I were riding in limos, and if I couldn't lay $400 on a ball game, then I couldn't see why I was here at all. True, I'd made it a point to steer clear of sports betting for the longest time, and this was nearly 10 percent of my tutorial stake, but this was the kind of twisted thinking I'd brought with me, like I was playing with house money—only in my case it really *was* house money, money I needed to pay for our new windows and our furniture and our heating bill.

I panicked, is the best I can figure it. I stepped from the elevator and saw this vast poker room, and I spun on my heels and made for the safety of the sports club. I couldn't face the poker tables just yet, needed the familiar feel of throwing good money after bad on a ball game in order to get comfortable. Then I stepped back out into the poker room, counted eighty tables before I lost track, and thought of the tiny poker rooms back in Tunica and wondered how I'd gotten in so far over my head. Only other Vegas casino I'd played in was the Bellagio, on two previous junkets to town, but the Horseshoe was a different kind of poker room. Twice the size of the Bellagio, easy, and a little worn and seedy by comparison. The place was in serious need of a face-lift and a steam cleaning. It was dark and dank, and even though they no longer allowed smoking in the main room, the place reeked of years and years of cigars and cigarettes. The smoke was in the carpets, in the drapes, in the seat cushions. It was all around.

There were two giant poker rooms, actually. Upstairs, Binion's was staging an endless series of preliminary World Series events. Seven-Card Stud. Omaha Hi/Lo. H.O.R.S.E. Ace to Five Triple-Draw Lowball. Pot-Limit Hold 'Em. Razz. You name it, they were playing it, with six-figure prize money and World Series bracelets to the winners. Men "The Master" Nguyen. Doyle Brunson. Amir Vahedi. I caught sight of Phil Hellmuth across the room, and I pointed him out to Bruce like he was Elvis—and in this world he was. There were top tournament players at every table. Players I recognized. Players I'd be sitting alongside once the tournament started. Players I didn't need to be sitting alongside just yet. Downstairs was for the amateurs and hopefuls and wannabes. It's funny, how there was a real class distinction in the way they had the place set up, upstairs and downstairs, but I'd never much cared about class, so I headed downstairs, where the action at the satellite tables and ring games was more my speed.

The satellite tables had $100 or $1,000 buy-ins and offered winners the chance to keep trading up for a $10,000 seat at the main event. If you already had a seat, like me, you could still play in these satellite tournaments—and if you managed to win one of the tables, you'd earn your prize money in chips that had no real cash value at the casino windows but which you could barter to other players looking to buy in to the tournament, at face value. If you didn't already have a seat in the main event, your winnings were automatically assigned to cover the buy-in at the next-level satellite.

Bruce and I did a quick study. We might have figured out a thing or two before arriving, but we couldn't think that far ahead. Our plan hadn't gone much beyond playing at some live tables. So we walked the room and learned what we could, quick as we could. At the $100 satellites, they started you out with about 500 in chips. At the $1,000 tables, they staked each player about 5,000 in chips, so there was a lot more poker to be played on the bigger-money tables. The general rule of thumb was that the bigger the money, the better the players, so you had to find a balance between the flexibility of all those chips and the degree of difficulty against all those stronger players. When you start with only 500 in chips, you're pretty much going all in whenever you have a hand. It's more of a crap shoot. When you start with 5,000 in chips, you can actually play some poker and bluff and try to read some people. There's more subtlety to the game. Happily, there were also tables in between—$300 and $500—but I knew I'd have to log some serious time on the $1,000 tables before the main event if I hoped to have any kind of chance.

So that's just what I did. As Maddux and the Braves and my $400 wager got the shit kicked out of them in Atlanta, I proceeded to get the shit kicked out of me at these satellite tables. First couple games I played, I was treading water. Couldn't catch any cards or any kind of momentum. Held my own for some long stretches and then crumbled like a house of cards. Eventually, though, I started to catch on some. I started to *get* how the live game was different from the virtual deal, how tournament play stood apart from a ring game, how I might actually make some noise in the main event if my money held out until then.

By the second day, I had things all figured out. Or I thought I had things all figured out, which was close enough to the same thing for the time being. I was up a couple hundred dollars in poker and down $400 to the Atlanta Braves, so the first move of the day was to lay another $400 on another baseball game, to get my money back. It was the kind of stupid, loss-chasing bet that got me into that ton of trouble with my offshore sports-club account all those years ago, but in my defense it's easy to forget these hard-earned lessons at a place like Binion's. It's easy to be seduced by the quick-money mentality that takes hold as soon as you land at the airport and walk by your first Vegas slot machine. It's all so *right there*.

The more I played, the more I learned. For one thing I learned that there are all kinds of side bets going at these tables. There's the straight action that flows through the dealer, and then there are things like "last-longer" bets—as in a side wager between a few players at the table to see who lasts longer, which can be an effective way to short your action and pull some money from the table even if you can't manage to win the whole damn thing. Sometimes, when you get down to two or three people, players will cut deals with each other to cover their butts. They'll carve up $10,000 three ways in a winner-share-all agreement—like those Poker Stars players were hoping to do when we got down to our final table.

I didn't know any of this kind of stuff went on in these live poker rooms, but I guess that's why I had gone out early, to figure it all out. I was up a little bit, and then I was down a little bit, and then, on the third afternoon, I threw still more money at a third baseball game—this time for $1,000. I played another $1,000 satellite table and lost that as well, and I did a small accounting in the middle of my third day of catch-up play and found myself down $3,000. Bruce and I were living like college kids, scarfing what we could at the free buffets that sprang up every here and there, eating on the cheap in a small snack bar in the poker room. We never left the casino. We were there to play poker, just, so that's what we did. That and blow a couple thousand bucks on some baseball games we couldn't even bother to watch and that seemed more than a little beside the point.

There was a Poker Stars reception the day or two leading up to the tournament, but we were too busy playing poker to peel ourselves away from the tables even for the free food. Too busy and too wildly indifferent. I learned later that there were thirty-seven seats in the main event being taken up by the winners of various Poker Stars tournaments, so the company had a fairly big presence at Binion's. There'd be T-shirts and hats we'd all have to wear during the tournament and other events as the week ground on, but there was too much for me to learn on those satellite tables to waste time meeting and greeting my fellow amateurs. At the very least, I meant to finish ahead of the thirty-six other Poker Stars players, and I wouldn't do that by hanging around at receptions. As long as my money was holding out, I'd stay at the tables.

All told, I got in a solid five days of poker before the main event—and I actually managed to win a couple tables. Won a couple last-longer bets, and cut up a grand prize or two, to where I was still sitting with about $1,500. Notice that I didn't write that I was *up* $1,500, but that I was still sitting with that amount, which meant that I had blown the other $3,000. But I convinced myself it was money, and time, well spent. Bruce was playing alongside me pretty often, or studying my game and helping me to spot my weaknesses. I didn't think I had any tells, but there they were, all over the damn place. I'd flare my nostrils when I bluffed. I'd hold my breath if I was nervous about another player's call. I'd check my hole cards twice when I was bluffing. Or I'd freeze on a draw.

I took notes as Bruce talked. The way to play it, I figured, was to do these things all the time, to mix them up in such a way that they had nothing to do with the cards I was playing. To hide behind my glasses and develop a stone-cold stare, no matter what I was playing. That way if a flared nostril got the better of me, no one would know what to make of it. That's how it is with tells—they're just an indication of nerves. It doesn't matter if you're itchy over a positive outcome or itchy over a negative outcome. I can be the same degree of nervous if I'm sweating out whether an opponent is going to call me when I *don't* have the cards as I am in sweating out whether an opponent is going to call me when I *do* have the cards. Nerves are nerves, and a good way to combat some of these unshakable tells is to always play a little bit nervous. That way you never give off anything. Or here's a better way to put it: You give off a ton, but no one can figure out what it all means.

I must have given off a ton at a $100 single-table satellite where I sat down to play midway through my tournament preliminaries. I was still looking to get my sea legs, but more and more I had started to feel as if I knew what I was doing—enough not to do anything stupid like go all in on the second hand of the satellite, but the second hand came around and I pushed all in with an ace-king, unsuited.

Let me take a step back for a moment and relay some of the relevant details of the first hand, because they'll come into play on my all-in move. We were playing with $5 chips, on the $5/$10 blind, and I was sitting in the seven seat. I was dealt two low cards and decided to fold. The guy on the small blind folded as well when the betting came back around to him, leaving him $5 short on the hand. Second hand, that guy in the two seat was now on the button when I was dealt that ace-king, and like an idiot I pushed all in. It really was a fool move—rash, hardheaded, inexperienced—and I knew better than to make it, but that didn't stop me. The blinds aren't big enough to justify a move like that, and there's no reason to risk everything right out of the gate, before you can even get a feel for the table. But it wouldn't be the only stupid move I'd make on this hand.

Everyone else folded but the button—the guy in the two seat who was short the $5 from his opening stack. He turned over a low pocket pair, and the community cards did nothing to change either of our hands, so he wound up winning the pot. And wiping me out on just the second hand of the satellite—or so I thought. I'd gone all in, with all of my original chips, against a guy who had yet to play a hand, so I pushed my chair from the table and started to walk away in search of another place to throw out my money.

I was pissed at myself for making such a dumb move, and I was not liking what it told me about what I still had to learn, but when I was a couple steps from the table, I heard the dealer call back to me. "Hey, buddy," I heard. "You forgot something."

He had my last remaining $5 chip in his hand, and he flipped it to me with his thumb, like something out of a movie. I was quick enough to catch it, which was better than having to scramble for it on the ratty casino carpet, but it was impossible to look cool after

walking away from the table like that. I'd forgotten that the guy on the button had already lost $5 as the small blind in the opening hand, so he had been unable to match my full-stack all-in bet on his call. The bet itself had been a stupid, rookie mistake, but here I had compounded it with another, and as I caught the chip from the dealer, I didn't know whether to smile at this small piece of good luck or to pretend the whole exchange didn't happen. I wasn't knocked out of this satellite after all. I still had a single chip left, and I sat back down hoping to make the best of it.

And I did. Played that chip immediately on a suited nine-three—the least intimidating all-in bet in the history of all-in bets. Caught another nine on the flop, and somehow the pair held up against four other players, and I pushed my stack to $25. I had no choice except to play those few chips recklessly, but the cards were with me. A high pair on one hand. A flush on another. A straight draw that didn't pan out but was enough to scare off the competition. In sum, a nice run of decent cards on consecutive hands, and pretty soon the talk at the table was all about how wild and funny it would be if I managed to recover with that one $5 chip, from walking away from the table after tanking that ace-king on the second hand of the tournament. It became the running joke of the morning, and the cards were in on it.

Wonder of wonders, I wound up winning the damn table—$1,000 in chips that I could now trade for hard cash. From that one lowly chip to the last man standing, on the back of some good cards and some ballsy moves that I probably wouldn't have made from a stronger position. All in the fallout from one fool move on top of another.

And here's another wonder: Folks were happy to lose to me, considering the circumstances. Well, maybe I'm overstating things a bit here for dramatic effect. No one is ever *happy* to lose at cards, but given that most of them had to lose anyway, and that most players become resigned to losing at some point before actually losing, they didn't seem to mind so much losing to me. Why? Because they weren't walking away empty-handed. They were walking away

with a story—about some kid with the unlikely name of Money-maker forgetting he still had a chip on the table and calling it quits, only to be summoned back by the dealer and to play that lone chip into the winning stack.

It was, for a brief chunk of that morning, the talk of the satellite tables, and as I moved to my next table, it occurred to me that this right here might be as good as it gets—and if that was the case, then this right here would have to be enough.

DAY ONE: LATE NIGHT ♥ ♣ ♠ ◆

Final session of the night, and our table was broken up at last. No way to tell if we were the only table still intact from the opening day of play, but I suspected we were. And I guessed that I had had enough. It was about ten o'clock, and I'd been playing with the same eight players since noon. I was tired and frazzled and a little punch-drunk with my early success, but at the same time, my game had become a little tired and frazzled and punch-drunk as well. There's a tendency to get complacent, I think, when you're at the same table with the same players for hours on end, especially when you're surrounded by conservative, defensive players. There's no heat to the action after such a long while, no urgency, and on the first day of a world-championship tournament, when there are dozens and dozens of tables with all kinds of heat and urgency, with hundreds and hundreds of players looking to win the whole damn tournament on one damn hand, you find yourself longing for an extra measure of excitement. You want a taste of what everyone else is having. Anyway, that's how I was feeling when the tournament directors finally scattered our seven remaining players to other tables. I was thinking, Hey, all right, it's about time.

It's funny how an early hand can establish a tone at a new table—and early hands don't come much earlier than the first. That's what happened here. Sat myself down at my new table in the back corner of the room, nodded hello to a bunch of players I didn't recognize, shook a couple hands, and began to stack my chips. It was a good-size stack—about 20,000—and I was hoping it made a good impression. Very first hand of the session, I drew pocket aces, and it was all I could do to keep from smiling. The odds of drawing pocket aces, the strongest opening hand in Hold 'Em, run about 220–1. I wasn't expecting them on my first hand, but here they ran right to me. I was sitting in the six seat. The dealer button was on the guy in the two seat. The blinds were getting steeper every two hours, and there was also an ante added to the game, from this round forward, as a means of accelerating play and raising the stakes at each table—starting here at 25 and going up each subsequent round. So by the time the call came around to me there was already a good-size pot in the middle of the table.

I called, thinking these players didn't know me to look at me, and if I made some kind of monstrous raise first time they heard my voice, they'd have likely thrown in their cards until they could get a fix on what kind of player I was. So I called. Best hand at the table, and I was playing possum.

The guy on the button made a substantial raise—2,000—and I immediately called. He was sitting behind about 10,000 in chips, so I had him two to one in chips, and unless he was holding the other two aces, I had him dead to rights in cards.

I called. Didn't give much thought to what the button was holding. I didn't really care. I had pocket aces. Of course I was gonna call.

Everyone else fell out of the hand, so it was just me and the button on the flop, which came down queen-three-seven. Nothing much for him to work with, unless he'd flopped a set on a pocket pair. No straight draw. No flush draw. Just me and my aces, looking good.

I checked.

Here again, I didn't want to come off as too eager. If I had any kind of history with these other players, I might have made some kind of bet, but I thought that with the way the button had bet so aggressively before the flop, there were still some chips to be shaved from his stack.

And then it happened—boom! The guy on the button moved all in. Another 8,000 or so in chips.

I thought, What the hell does he have? I hadn't put him on a pocket pair before the flop, although maybe he'd caught a set of threes or sevens. Pocket queens and he'd probably have bet bigger than 2,000 to start. Most likely he was sitting with an ace-queen, king-queen, or a queen-jack, which would give him high pair on the board and a strong kicker, which in turn would justify his aggressive move. It was also possible he was playing a queen-three or a queen-seven, even though those wouldn't explain his opening bet. The more I thought about it, though, the more I saw there wasn't much to think about. I had pocket aces. I had to call this guy. If I was wrong, I'd still have about 10,000 in chips. I'd still be able to last out the night if I played it conservative. And if I was right, I'd put him out of the tournament, add a mess of chips to my stack, and make a tremendous first impression at this new table.

I called.

First major decision of the tournament for me, and it was really a no-brainer. You have pocket aces, you call.

The guy on the button flipped over ace-queen. Top pair with an ace. That explained his move.

He wasn't happy to see my two aces, I'll tell you that.

A king came on the turn and a two on the river, and I had knocked out my first opponent.

And then a strange thing happened. As I was restacking my chips and trying not to smile too broadly, I noticed a slightly overweight guy with an ESPN badge pointing at me from across the room. He was close enough that I could hear him say to the guy standing next to him, "This kid right here." As if he'd been pointing me out for some unknown reason. The two of them kept talking and pointing at me and making notes and nodding.

I leaned over to the player on my right, in the eight seat, and said, "Any idea who that is?"

"That's Lou Diamond," the other player said, as if the man's name would reveal all.

"Who's Lou Diamond?" I wanted to know.

"Some handicapper," the guy said. "Big poker guy. Covering the tournament for ESPN, I think."

I considered this information and thought, What the hell is that about? Really, there were camera crews all around the floor, but they had been focused on the main television table and the few outer tables where there were big-name players. Up until now none of those cameras had been pointed at me—and, far as I could tell, nobody's finger had been pointed at me either. I'd just assumed I was sailing along under everyone's radar, going about my business, minding my own—even though, I suppose, in going about my own business, I was getting close to keeping some of these other players from going about theirs.

I didn't catch anything in the way of cards next couple hands, and soon as I had a chance, I stood and stretched my legs. Wandered over to where Lou Diamond and this other ESPN guy were standing. I didn't care if I missed a few hands. The dealer would post my blinds and pull my antes, but I had a cushion. I had over 30,000 in chips, and there was nobody at the table I was too worried about, and this guy pointing at me saying, "This kid right here," had set me on edge. This was my main worry at just that moment. I didn't like it when people I didn't know started talking about me. Left me feeling maybe I had done something wrong or that they might somehow have it in for me.

Lou Diamond was standing by himself when I crossed to him and introduced myself. I said, "Hey. Chris Moneymaker. How you doin'?" He shook my hand, and I kept talking before he could get a word in. "I saw you pointing at me. I'm wondering, is something wrong? Did I do something wrong?"

"No, no, no," Lou Diamond assured me. "Not at all." He told me who he was, told me he was working the floor for ESPN, monitoring the field to see how the players were doing. "It's just I've been watching you play. You're having some first day. I was pointing at you because you're my dark horse to win the whole tournament."

Here I'd been thinking this guy was gonna bounce me from the floor for holding my cards wrong or something, and he was picking me as his dark horse. I thought, Wow! I think I even said it: "Wow!"

"Picked the last couple winners last couple years," he explained. "Usually I've got a favorite and a dark horse, and right now you're my

dark horse." He couldn't have been nicer about it—although I'm guessing he could have been a real shit, but if he told me he was picking me to win the tournament, I'd have still thought he was a really nice guy.

"Me?" I said, making sure.

He nodded.

"Hey, man, thanks," I said.

"Nothing to thank me for," he said. "You're playing well."

I thanked him again for the kind words and returned to the table. I'd been away only a few minutes, but it felt like forever. I'd gone from being a no-name, no-account amateur to the dark-horse favorite of a well-known handicapper, and it takes a while to get back from something like that.

But I got back to it soon enough. Started talking some with a few of the players at the table. There was a woman seated across from me, next to a guy wearing a Late Night Poker T-shirt, first woman I'd played with so far in the tournament. (There were thirty women in the opening field of 839—and Annie Duke, sister of "The Professor," Howard Lederer, would be the last woman standing, in forty-seventh place, earning $20,000 in runner-up prize money.) I didn't know it at the time, but the woman across from me was Thithi Tran, known on the tour as "Mimi," and she'd made it to the final table in the Seven-Card Stud event of the World Series just a couple weeks earlier. A real formidable player—outside of Dan Harrington, probably the top player I'd face all day, at least in terms of reputation. She asked what the deal was with Poker Stars, and I filled her in, and we talked for a bit, waiting on our hands.

With over 30,000 in chips and time running out on the first day of play, I could afford to be patient. What I couldn't afford was to do anything stupid—and after another hour or so, patient hit hard into stupid. I was on the small blind. Wasn't planning to even look at my cards until the bet came back around to me. The guy on the button, same guy who'd identified Lou Diamond for me, bet 1,500—a relatively small bet this late in the first day, especially when you're sitting behind a stack like mine, but still a good chunk of chips.

I looked at my cards: pocket sevens. I called. I wasn't planning on getting mixed up in anything I couldn't handle, but I wanted to see where this was going. I don't care how big the stakes were or how important it was to me to last out this first day—I wasn't used to mucking pocket sevens before the flop.

The big blind called.

Everyone else folded.

The flop: seven-jack-three.

Another set for the dark horse, and there was nothing else out there, so I decided to bet 2,000 into it. My strategy kept changing with the situation, and this time I felt that from my strong chip position, I could afford to push the guy on the button a little, all the time hoping he would come over the top with a raise of his own, sweeten the pot that much more. We were about even in chips at the start of the hand, but I didn't think we were even in cards. He'd shown himself to be an aggressive player, so I thought there were more chips to be taken on the hand.

The big blind folded.

And, as I hoped, the button came over the top. Big time. Raised me 10,000 and got me all kinds of excited. I was putting him on a stone-cold bluff. Ace-king. Ace-jack. One of those hopeful hands.

I called, feeling certain I had this guy beat.

It was shaping up to be the biggest hand of the tournament that I'd gotten involved in, but I had a comfortable chip position and the clock was winding down on the first day of play. I'd make it until tomorrow either way, although I wasn't counting on losing the hand.

The turn card was a five.

I checked, wanting to see what this guy would do.

He thought about it a beat, and then he went all in. I wasn't expecting such a bold move, not with the cards on the table. Second time in two playable hands someone had pushed me all in—only this time the guy pushing me was about even in chips, which on the short end would have put me all but out of the tournament.

I thought, Okay, what do I do? What do I do? What do I do? With this move I was putting the guy on pocket jacks, worst case for me, but then I thought, with the hard-charging way he'd been playing, he would *have made a bigger move before the flop if he had pocket jacks. He could have gut-shotted a straight, but I didn't think so with the way he'd played the hand so far. I was pissed, a little, that this guy had pushed me to this moment of indecision, when my plan had been to sit back and pick my spots. But then I realized, Hey, if I'm picking my spots, here I am with a set of sevens. This was as good a spot as any.*

At one point, while I was trying to figure my next move, I actually stood up, pulled off my shades, and stepped away from my seat. I looked at the guy on the button and said, "Do you have those jacks, buddy?" I asked real nicely, too, on the off chance he'd give something away with his response. Something in his expression. Something in his body language. Something. Then I thought, Aw, hell. If he has jacks, he has jacks. That was the only hand that could beat me, but I wasn't playing against the only hand that could beat me. I was playing against whatever it was this guy was likely holding. And risking the whole tournament in the bargain.

I decided to call. I stood up again, turned to my right, and said, "I think you have jacks, but I'm gonna call."

The guy in the three seat, who hadn't made a real move since we were sitting here, threw up his hands in disgust, like he couldn't believe I was moving all in if I was putting the other guy on the strongest hand.

The guy on the button flipped over pocket aces, liking his chances while I was liking mine even more. I never thought I'd be so happy to see my opponent turn over pocket aces.

I flipped over my pocket sevens, and he liked his chances a little less. My sevens were good.

And they were even better after another jack came on the river. My full house beat the crap out of his two pair, and I'd put the guy out and doubled up in chips just before the close of play.

The guy in the three seat was practically scratching his head—not liking my balls or my banter, apparently. "If you put him on jacks, why'd you call him?" he said. "Makes no sense."

"Guess it doesn't," I admitted, still trying to catch my breath from the hand. "Maybe I'm stupid."

"No, really," he persisted. "Why'd you call?"

The guy was all but ripshit. He had next to nothing in chips. I had the kind of stack that wins prizes. He had me flying blind—worse, flying deaf, dumb, and blind—and raking it in just the same. I had him on frustrated, so I chose to ignore the question and concentrate on counting my chips, which is a good thing to do when you're the only player at the table with chips that merit concentration. Sixty thousand of them, give or take. Next-closest stack was probably Mimi Tran's, at about 15,000.

Couple hands later some of the players got moved around as more and more players were knocked out, and Johnny Chan wound up sitting at the table next to me, in such a way that we were almost back-to-back. Realize, when Johnny Chan moved about the room, a whole mess of folks followed. Camera guys. Sound guys. Commentators. Handicappers like Lou Diamond. Fans hoping for a better seat along the rail to observe his action. I looked up at all that movement and watched as one of the greatest poker players that ever lived took his seat among this new group, set out his chips, and placed down that weird orange he's always sniffing. Funkiest-looking orange I've ever seen. People say he's had the same orange for years, and I wouldn't doubt it from the looks of it. Anyway, our backs were almost touching, which made it difficult to peer over my shoulder and stare too closely at Johnny Chan without making it obvious that I was peering over my shoulder and staring too closely at Johnny Chan, so I kinda darted my eyes back and forth. I'd made enough rookie mistakes already, and I would no doubt make a bunch more, but, not wanting to appear starstruck or out of my element, I checked him out with these sidelong glances, hoping no one would notice. On one of these glances, I picked up that his stack was nothing like mine. Not even close. And I thought, That's Johnny Chan, man, and he's got nothing on me.

CHIP LEADERS: CLOSE OF PLAY, DAY ONE ♥♣♠♦

Player	Chip Count
1. Greenstein, Barry	94,775
2. Hollink, Rob	71,900
3. Farha, Sam	71,255
4. Benvenitsi, Tomer	70,650
5. Jacobs, Tom	70,600
6. Ivey, Phillip	66,600
7. Thorson, Olof	64,400
8. Deeb, Kassam Ibrahim	63,575
9. Watkins, Bryan	63,000
10. Deknijff, Martin	60,575
11. MONEYMAKER, CHRIS	60,475
12. Nguyen, Scotty	60,050
13. Jenson, Ood Erlend	60,000
14. Lester, Jason	55,125
15. Awada, Yehia	54,925
16. Hellmuth, Phil	54,775
17. Giordano, Peter	54,650
18. Klinger, Josef	54,175
19. Nguyen, Men "The Master"	53,675
20. Sarcone, James	52,750

PLAYERS REMAINING: 385

5.
DAY TWO

The poker player learns that sometimes both
science and common sense are wrong; that
the bumblebee can fly; that, perhaps, one should
never trust an expert; that there are more things
in heaven and earth than are dreamt of by those
with an academic bent.

—David Mamet
"Things I Have Learned Playing Poker
on the Hill," *Writing in Restaurants*

I was too tired to celebrate lasting out the first day of play. Too tired to grab a beer or something to eat. Too tired to call my dad or Kelly and give them a report. Man, I was too tired to do anything but crash. I was fried, really. Twelve hours of turbocharged poker, up against world-class players . . . it drains you, and I was a couple hours past empty.

Sleep was about all I could handle—and even that would soon get a little out of hand.

Nine o'clock the next morning, Bruce shook me awake with the standings sheets from the night before. We didn't even know they posted these things, but here was Bruce, waving a list of the chip leaders and table assignments like they held the keys to the next round of play. And, for a lot of players, they did. Folks waited up until two o'clock in the morning, sometimes as late as three, until the sheets were posted, to get a first read on who they'd be playing with the next day, where they'd be sitting, how their stack measured up against the rest of the field. In a knockout tournament where everyone was looking for some kind of edge, the sheets were like currency—only we didn't know enough to seek them out.

Bruce was more excited than I was to look at the leader board, where I was listed in eleventh chip position after the first day of play. I was too thrashed to get terribly excited about anything, but it registered that I'd had a better day than 828 other players—that is, if you measure success in a marathon Hold 'Em tournament by chip count instead of mere survival. Going in, caught up in all that doubt and indecision, I had moments when I worried I might just be the 839th-weakest player in the field, and already I'd outlasted 454 of them and was well positioned against all the rest. I thought, Damn, if that don't beat all. I'd been hoping simply to last out the first day of play, and I'd somehow managed to build a commanding stake instead. Ahead of Scotty Nguyen. Ahead of Phil Hellmuth. Ahead of Amir Vahedi, Howard Lederer, Johnny Chan.

Ahead of my wildest dreams.

"Not too bad," I said, handing the sheets back to Bruce and slamming back down onto my pillow. I was asleep again in the five seconds I'd pledged to wait out each move at the tables.

Woke up three hours later like it was no time at all. The digital clock by my bed said it was 12:05 P.M.—five minutes past the start of the second day of play, which I immediately took to mean five minutes past any chance I had of continuing in the Series. I bolted upright. I thought, Shit, I've missed the damn tournament. Slept right through it, like an idiot. I hadn't thought to set an alarm, or to leave a wake-up call, or to ask Bruce to wake me. It never occurred to me I'd sleep this late—who the hell sleeps until noon?—and now, as I slapped myself awake and splashed some cold water on my face, it appeared I'd blown right past my chances. I couldn't believe it. I had no idea how the tournament organizers would react to this bedraggled amateur stumbling down to the poker room a full fifteen minutes after the start of play. I wondered if blowing off those first couple hands was grounds for disqualification. I thought, Well, wouldn't that just suck, to come this far and throw away such a great first day because I'd overslept? It would be the all-time king of self-destructive moves and the biggest bonehead play in the history of the World Series.

There was no time to shower. I don't think I even brushed my teeth. (Sorry, guys, if you caught the seat next to me at the opening table.) Just threw on the same khaki pants from the day before, dug a clean white Poker Stars shirt from the gear the organizers had given me on check-in, and raced downstairs like a dead man running. Really, I thought I was done, and that Bruce and I would be sent packing, and that I'd have to get a good drunk on before heading back to Nashville and having to explain myself to everyone I knew.

The check-in tables were mostly empty when I raced across the lobby to the main poker room. Everyone was inside, on the tournament floor, monitoring the action. I found someone in charge and began to make apologies, thinking I'd have to sweet-talk my way back in, but the person just handed me my Baggied chips and directed me to my first table. I'd missed a couple hands, was all. Happens all the time. In fact, they were still waiting on a few players to check in for the second round, so I wasn't even the worst offender. And there wasn't even any penalty for my small offense; the dealer would have posted my blinds and my antes, and someone would adjust my chips accordingly once I sat down.

What had seemed a great big deal on the long elevator ride downstairs turned out to be no big deal after all. Still, not exactly the way I wanted to start the second day of play. A couple pounds short of prepared—and looking like such a complete sack of shit that I supposed I fit right in. Hard-core poker players, up all night and round the clock, are not exactly slaves to fashion and hygiene, so I guess I was about as disheveled and unkempt as the next guy. A lot of these folks had probably kept playing, all night long, straight through to our noon start, and I convinced myself that at least I had to look a sight better than them.

Bruce flashed me a *Where the hell have you been?* look from behind the rail as I moved to Table 57, seat six—my opening position for the day. I shrugged as in a sheepish apology and sat myself down. The other players barely looked up from their chips and their cards as I made ready to play, and as I scanned the table, I realized I didn't recognize anyone. I also realized that I should have spent some time studying the sheets, to learn what I could about the folks I'd be playing with, but there wasn't a single familiar face—save for that of Mimi Tran, the woman who'd been at my table the night before, who was now in seat four, two seats to my right. She started the day with 14,225 in chips, which put her somewhere at the low end for our table. I had been the high stack at the start of play, with 60,475, trailed by two strong players I'd never heard of at the time—Chris Grigorian, with 33,775 in chips, and Ken Lennard, at 25,850.

I watched Grigorian play a couple hands before jumping in and decided I'd do well not to get mixed up with him. Mimi Tran, too, seemed to know her way around the table. You don't see a whole lot of women playing poker in the casinos, and there had been only thirty women in the opening field of the tournament, so I took the time to consider how having a woman at the table might change the run of play. A lot of times, you'll see weaker players try to bully a female at the table, same way they bullied the few of us who'd earned our seats through some promotion or other, but Mimi Tran looked like she was up to anything these guys could throw at her. Doubled up her stack before too long, made a couple of ballsy plays, but then the two of us locked heads on a hand that would fall my way.

I was dealt pocket fives.

She was dealt ace-king, unsuited.

She made a big bet.

I called.

The flop came down nine-seven-six, which, as far as I knew at the time, gave us each a straight draw.

She moved all in.

Now, ace-king is a killer opening hand, but it's something less than killer after a low flop, so she'd clearly overbet her hand. Before the flop it's not a bad bet; after the flop it doesn't make a whole lot of sense. I had her about four to one in chips, so I called.

The turn was a deuce.

The river was a queen.

My fives were good, and Mimi Tran was put out—all on a too-aggressive move that I bet she wishes she could take back.

That hand put me over 100,000 in chips for the first time in the tournament, but I gave some of them back soon afterward, and things went on in this up-and-down way for the next while, to where I was soon enough down to the same 80,000 or so in chips that I'd had before the hand with Mimi Tran. I was still the chip leader at our table, but I'd given back a good deal of my strong position.

It took a while, really, for me to get all the way into this second day of play. There was the distraction earlier, with me running late, and I started out tentative, letting some of the other folks at the table call the shots. For every strong hand I played, I let myself get pushed around on another—and for the most part, I was doing only slightly better than treading water. Again, not exactly the way I wanted to start the second day, but I told myself that as long as I was still alive, it was okay.

Late in the afternoon, we were told to race off all of our green chips—which basically meant we had to trade in our green $25 chips for the black $100 chips. The antes and blinds had gotten to where we no longer needed the $25 chips, and it was far easier for the house and for the players to track the bigger-denomination chips as the pots grew. It's a fairly routine point of pause, in every high-stakes tournament—only in my case this was my first tournament, so it was all new to me. The deal was, we were supposed to keep playing as we were counting out our chips, and because my stack stood taller than most, I was doing an awful lot of counting. Players started throwing their green chips to me, asking me to make change, and the whole process went on for a couple hands. For the most part, I was folding my cards, just to keep track of all my chips, wanting to make sure I didn't shortchange myself. The hands kept coming, but I tried to finish up the chip maintenance, best I could.

During all of this chip counting and change making with the house and the other players, I was dealt a suited ace-ten, and I reckoned maybe I could do two things at once. I thought, Hell, it's like walking and chewing gum at the same time. Can't be that difficult. I liked to focus my full attention on each hand, but it was tough to look away from a suited ace-ten just to do this little piece of housekeeping, so when the guy in the two seat made a raise, I figured I'd call. I figured, What the hell.

Now, there were so many holes and shifts in my tournament strategy that it's probably a stretch to even call it a strategy, but my general rule of thumb, first two days of the tournament, was to stay away from hands when someone in an earlier position was betting strong into me. I'd steer clear unless I had a real hand—a pocket pair or something stronger than a simple pair if the bet came after the flop. That's the way I'd been playing. Unless I was the one doing the raising and making the action, I wasn't much interested in calling off someone else's bet. Ace-ten, suited, was a nice enough opening hand, but it was nothing special in this tournament, and if I had stuck to my general rule, I'd have mucked the hand. Online? Who knows, I probably would have played those cards, especially from my strong chip position. At our regular local game back home in Nashville? Sure, I'd give those cards a ride. But at the World Series of Poker, deep into the second day of play, I felt I needed something stronger in order to respond.

That said, I responded anyway. I was distracted by this business with the chips and feeling like I hadn't played a hand in a long while and thinking I could manage to play these cards and count my chips at the same time. So I called.

Another ten came on the flop, along with two low cards, and it now looked like I could steal the hand, but this guy bet into me again, big. I thought, Well, what is he playing? I had high pair on the board, with an ace kicker, so I put him on a high pocket pair—maybe queens or jacks. That would explain his strong opening bet.

I don't know why, but I called. Waited out my five seconds and called. I knew better, but I couldn't help myself. I had this guy about two to one in chips, but I also felt I had him on a strong hand, and my head was all over the place, and the whole table was in this mini state of chaos. I was really just reacting to the run of play, more than anything else. That's a dangerous position to be in against a strong player, and at the World Series of Poker, I had to assume that everyone across the table from me was a strong player.

The turn was another low card.

He bet big again.

I called again, still for no good reason but that I was already into it.

A king came on the river, which didn't do anything for me but could have done a whole lot for my nemesis in the two seat, who fired into the pot again. Another big bet.

I set down my chips and stopped with the counting. I looked at my pocket cards a second time. I looked across the table at my opponent. Hadn't really noticed him until just this moment, but he was wearing a Late Night Poker shirt, so I pegged him for another promotional satellite winner, same as me. I considered my cards and wished like hell I hadn't gotten mixed up in this kind of hand. I thought, What in the world am I doing? I'd already donated about 25,000 in chips to this one pot, and here I was thinking about donating 15,000 more. Half my stack. On what? I no longer thought I could actually win the hand, not after that king on the river. I suppose I could have raised and tried to scare him off with a steep bet, but he was just about all in as it was, and if he was any kind of player, he would have put me on nothing more than that pocket ten, from the way I'd been betting.

And so, like an idiot, I called, on the confused theory that I'd paid this guy off this far and I might as well pay him off the rest of the way.

He turned over a five-king. One of the low cards on the flop had been a five, and that low pair was all he'd been playing until he caught that king. The river had made his hand and sunk mine.

We went to break immediately following the hand, and my first thought was, Why couldn't we wait until the break to race off those green chips? We could have kept playing without the distraction and counted out the chips on our fifteen-minute bathroom break. My next thought was, What the hell was I doing? And finally there was this: I'm in so far over my head I might drown.

I stepped outside for some fresh air and called Kelly on my cell phone. Told her it looked like I'd be coming home soon. Told her I'd just lost 40,000 in chips on a hand I shouldn't even have been playing and that I'd gone from the chip leader at my table to the middle of the pack, all on the heels of a fool move.

Just then some guy wandered over like he knew me. Turned out he did. He was Lou Diamond's sidekick from the day before, handicapping the field for ESPN. He happened to overhear my conversation with Kelly and stood off to the side waiting for me to finish the call. By this point I had figured out who he was and how I knew him. He was a young guy, looked to be about the same age as me, with a mustache and goatee to match my own. He walked over to me and put his hand on my shoulder. "Don't beat yourself up over it," he said.

"I'm playing stupid," I said, dejected as all get-out.

"I saw the hand," he said. "I'm watching you. Just forget about it. Chalk it up to experience."

He took me down the street to a little deli and bought me a hot dog and a Coke, to try to get my mind off the tournament for a beat or two. I ate about half the hot dog and then I felt like I was going to be sick. I felt like I had thrown the tournament away, and I said as much.

"You haven't thrown anything away," he assured me. "You're going to be fine. Just go back in there and start playing your game."

It was like something out of a Disney movie, the way this guy swept in like some guardian angel and tried to talk me down from my dejection and pump me back up. And he did a good job of it, too. Really calmed me down, helped me to get my mind back around the tournament, the other players at the table, what I'd need to do to rebuild my position. I didn't know this guy beyond his reputation as a handicapper, and he didn't know me beyond mine as Lou Diamond's dark horse, but he did a real nice thing that day, and I'll always be grateful.

I stayed outside with this guy for ten minutes or so beyond the break, still working on my focus, still trying to return to calm. I finally went back inside when I realized that the tournament directors must be thinking of me as some upstart prima donna, the way I'd blown off the start of play earlier that afternoon, the way I was blowing off these few hands here, but I figured I'd do better to sit out until my head was back on straight than to sit down before I was ready to play.

I returned to Table 57 determined to grind it out, to build back my stack, to continue to play with the kind of focus and grit that had served me so well the previous day. In the shifting hunches that passed for my tournament strategy, I decided to come out super-aggressive, to try to take control of the table. As it happened, I didn't move from Table 57 for the entire day, but folks kept filling our empty seats as players were eliminated around the room, so there was a lot of turnover, and I tried to pick on each new player as soon as he sat down. I tried to set the tone for the table, and over the next couple hours, I managed to build my stack up to 180,000 or so in chips, mostly by stealing some blinds and big-footing my way into hands against weaker stacks. Knocked a mess of smaller stacks from the tournament on nothing hands. I didn't really get mixed up

in any kind of major showdowns for the rest of the afternoon, leading all the way to the dinner break, just steadily and stealthily
added to my stack and let the other players beat each other up. It
hadn't been my strategy going in, but it was definitely a strategy.
Sometimes the cards dictate how you should play, and here the
cards were telling me to push on the front end, to hang back if we
were meant to see the flop. I was going by the cards and by my new
deli guru, whose name I never did catch.

And then, just before dinner, there was a pretty significant buzz
about our table, as Johnny Chan was moved over to fill a vacant seat.
Back-to-back World Series champion Johnny Chan. Poker legend
Johnny Chan. Widely regarded as the most complete poker player on
the tour Johnny Chan. *Rounders* Johnny Chan—God, me and my
buddies wore out that DVD. He had his trademark rancid orange
with him, and he had a nice pile of chips, and he also brought with
him a good number of folks in the gallery who seemed determined to
follow him throughout the tournament. Some of these guys, they're
like Tiger Woods at the U.S. Open, the way the pack follows them
from table to table, and Johnny Chan probably had the biggest following of all. Suddenly Table 57 went from being this anonymous
little outpost where I could push around under-the-radar players
like myself in relative peace and quiet to a front-and-center cir-
cus where the consummate poker player and his loyal fans would
now call the shots.

I sought out Bruce from my position across the room, and
when our eyes met, he mouthed Chan's name—*Johnny Chan!*—like
we were shooting hoops in our driveway and Michael Jordan just
happened by and we couldn't believe it. Oh, man, it was so completely cool, like a poker fantasy camp, to trade calls with a living,
breathing, orange-sniffing legend, but at the same time it was also
so completely chilling—and intimidating—to have to match this guy
heads up. I was the chip leader, by a big margin, and I was sure he'd
come out gunning for me.

I knew that my hands were numbered.

That's the thing about Johnny Chan, I quickly learned. When he sits down at a table, it's his table. Doesn't matter if you've had your way with these same players, past couple hours. Doesn't matter if you're sitting on a nice chip lead. All of that changes when he starts playing—and you become fresh meat, same as everyone else. In fact, you become the biggest target, because he sets his sights on the biggest stack and goes to work on it straight off. And that's just what he did. He was all kinds of confident and all business. He didn't give off a single thing. He bets, and he bets, and he bets, and it's all but impossible to put him on a hand. There's always small talk and banter at these tables, but very little of it comes from Johnny Chan. The only time I heard him say anything, outside of his betting, was when one of the roving cameramen happened by our table and he'd give a thumbs-up and shout, "See you at the final table, baby." That was the extent of his personality. I tried to joke with him a little, just to ease my own tensions and see if I could get some kind of reaction out of him, but he wouldn't have any of it. I asked him what the deal was with that orange of his, and he looked at me like I had sprouted horns. "It's just an orange," he said, flat, and I thought, Okay, it's just an orange. A lot of these guys have their odd little quirks and routines and good-luck charms to keep them company at the tables. There's nothing unusual about a grown man who carries the same orange from tournament to tournament, from table to table, just to sniff at it and roll it around and fiddle with it.

He wasn't about small talk and banter. Some players, that's a part of their game, but Johnny Chan was all about the action. He kept moving in on every damn hand, pushing and pushing, like he had it coming. And everybody kept laying down to him. We were like his punching bags, and after only an hour or so, he had taken a serious bite out of my stack. Took a big bite or two from just about everybody, whether they meant to go up against him or not. There was one run of hands in there, he pushed all in six times in a row. Six consecutive hands, and one or two of them against me. I'd never seen anything like it. Granted, I hadn't played a whole lot of tournament poker (hell, I hadn't played *any* tournament poker up until this week), but no one at the table had seen a run like this. Bam! Bam! Bam! And then—bam! three times more. It reminded me of that flurry of all-in hands in the Poker Stars tournament I'd won to get here, only there those moves seemed more reckless. Here they were bullying. And relentless. And the rest of us at the table had no choice but to get out of Chan's way.

And then, to make matters worse, there was another buzz around our table just before we were to break for the night. This time the commotion was for Phil Ivey, another top player. I'd never heard of Phil Ivey before the tournament, but after a few days at Binion's I'd heard enough. He was the talk of the room, the one to watch, the guy you didn't want to come up against, especially if he had a pile of chips in front of him. He was a young black guy, about the same age as me, given to wearing oversize basketball jerseys. No shades. No hat. Just an open, honest face that was about as difficult to read as *War and Peace,* and a lot of these handicappers were picking him to win the tournament. The book on Ivey was that he was probably the most dangerous player in the room behind a decent stack of chips.

It was such a huge comedown, to have had this table all to myself all afternoon, to have built up this nice chip position and a nice bullying reputation among these few players, and to now have to sit back and have Phil Ivey and Johnny Chan beat the same shit out of me. I was completely lost. I'd bet, they'd raise. I'd raise, they'd reraise. They were just running all over the table and running all over me—Ivey especially, once he sat down. I don't think I played a hand past the flop for the rest of the night, as I watched these guys whittle my stack from about 180,000 to just over 100,000. They bet like they had the nuts every time out, so I believed that they did. I couldn't pick up a tell for the life of me, and I couldn't pull off a bluff of my own if my tournament life depended on it—which, I was beginning to realize, it absolutely did. I was drawing some decent cards, caught some pocket pairs every once in a while, but I couldn't make anything out of them.

On one hand I was dealt pocket sixes and figured I would make a move, but Ivey kept coming over the top on me. I finally said something about it. I said, "Well, hell, you can't have a hand every time." And I called.

The flop was all high cards, so I checked.

Ivey bet big again, and I had to throw in my cards. I simply couldn't keep pace. Each hand would have cost me 30,000 or 40,000 in chips, just to get a look at his cards, and I didn't think I could afford it. Ivey even beat up on Chan a little bit as we pulled close to midnight. Started coming over the top on him, pushing him off of hands he seemed to want to play.

I'm telling you, the stroke of midnight, or whenever it was that the tournament directors were planning to pull the plug on this second day of play, couldn't come fast enough, and when it finally did, I slumped down in my chair. I didn't move for the longest time. Everyone was getting up and milling about and bagging their chips and checking in with folks they knew at some of the other tables, but all I could do was sit there and try to catch my breath. I felt like I'd taken a few rides too many on one of those killer roller coasters.

Bruce finally walked over to me. "Hey, Money," he said. "Rough day, huh?"

"Bruce, man," I said, "I think I'm a little bit outclassed. Ivey and Chan, they're pretty damn good."

"No shit," he said. "Kicked your ass pretty good."

Then we both laughed, and I felt somewhat better. Still felt like shit, but good enough to laugh.

I'd decided earlier that day to stick around for the late-night sheets, get an early indication who I'd be playing with tomorrow, see where I stood in chips, so we had a couple hours to kill before the things were posted. The plan had been to stay away from any kind of alcohol for the run of the tournament, to keep sharp, but

I hadn't counted on such a brutal ass-whipping and figured I needed a couple beers to wind down. So we walked across the street from the Horseshoe to a seedy strip club. Bruce worked the room like a politician, telling the girls that I was over at the Horseshoe making a move in the World Series of Poker, but they could not have cared less. He didn't have any money to slip into their G-strings, just this lame line of talk about his poker-playing buddy, and they'd heard every lame line of talk, every damn day. But we had our beers, and I got my mind off the tournament for the next while, got to where I was able to think, Hey, I'm still hanging in there. I'm still sitting with some chips. I've still got a shot at some kind of money.

Went back across the street to Binion's about two o'clock in the morning to see about the sheets, and there was Johnny Chan, assigned to my table again—this time seated two seats to my left. I thought, Damn, that sucks. I won't be able to steal any blinds. I won't be able to make a move without Johnny Chan sitting on top of me. And then there was Howard Lederer, positioned three seats to my right. One of the chip leaders so far in the tournament, considered one of the smartest players on the circuit, high stack at our table by a big margin. All around, players were checking out their table assignments, counting themselves lucky or unlucky, and I figured I was screwed.

If I could have stomped my feet and sulked and still managed to look cool doing it, I would have. I thought it was about the worst table assignment I could have drawn, but then I realized that this deep into the tournament, there *were* no easy tables. There were only 111 players left, and we were getting down to the best of the best, and I couldn't expect to be seated next to players like that Paradise Poker guy from my opening table. That wasn't how it worked.

I took the long way upstairs to my room, through the casino floor, and I happened to walk past a guy named Dan Goldman, the Poker Stars marketing guy. He was sitting at one of the poker tables playing a $1/$2 no-limit game. It was three o'clock in the morning, so I walked over to say hello. As the tournament went on, the Poker Stars people became more and more interested in how I was doing. There were thirty-seven of us who'd won seats going in, and at this point there were only four or five of us left, so the company was pretty pumped about our success. They couldn't have been nicer or more solicitous, because my good run was now tied in to them. Me and a guy named Olof Thorson had the two biggest stacks in the Poker Stars camp, and it was a big deal to these guys that we were doing well. We were wearing their shirts and hats at the table. We were helping them to achieve a real presence at the tournament. The longer we lasted, the smarter a guy like Dan Goldman would look to his bosses.

I showed Dan the seat assignments for the next day, thinking he might know a little more about these players than Bruce and I did.

"What do you think?" I said.

He studied the list, then slapped a hand to his bald head. "My God!" he exclaimed. "This is some table."

This was about the last thing I needed to hear.

He went over the list. Paul Darden, in the nine seat, one of the most respected players on the circuit. Brian Haveson, between me and Johnny Chan in the two seat, another strong player. Howard Lederer. Johnny Chan.

"It's the table from hell," he said.

I thought, Great.

Before heading back to my room, I went up to the Poker Stars suite to pick up some more gear to wear to my slaughter. Another couple shirts, another hat, a jacket. The deal was, the longer we lasted in the tournament, the better the gear they asked us to wear. I was going to get killed, but at least I'd look good.

It was probably about three-thirty in the morning when we got back up to our room, and Bruce and I were probably about six or seven beers to the good, and I figured I'd call my dad back in Knoxville, to give him a report. It was five-thirty in the morning back home, and I thought I'd catch him getting ready for work.

"I'm still alive," I said. "Still hanging in."

"Fill me in," he said.

And I did. Told him how I'd bullied my way to the chip lead at my table late in the afternoon. Told him how I'd been bullied back down later that night by Phil Ivey and Johnny Chan. Told him how I was looking at the table from hell tomorrow morning, with Johnny Chan on my left.

"Gonna be a tough run, then," he said.

"More like a war zone," I said.

"Just hang in there," he said. "Stay on your game. And wait for your damn cards."

"Yes, sir," I said.

"Make it through tomorrow," my father said, "and I'll come out on Thursday, cheer you on home."

"Sounds like a plan," I said.

CHIP LEADERS: CLOSE OF PLAY, DAY TWO ♥ ♣ ♠ ♦

Player	Chip Count
1. Vahedi, Amir	303,400
2. Watkins, Bryan	247,900
3. Nguyen, Scotty	214,300
4. Lederer, Howard	204,800
5. Deeb, Kassam Ibrahim	194,900
6. Ivey, Phillip	163,500
7. Luske, Marcel	156,800
8. Brenes, Humberto	152,200
9. Meehan, James	148,700
10. Boyd, Dutch	144,700
11. Hoang, Chuc	143,700
12. Hellmuth, Phil	139,100
13. Johnson, Timothy	130,800
14. Grigorian, Chris	121,900
15. Vinas, Tommy	119,800
16. Kaplan, Jonathan	119,100
17. Waterman, Dennis	117,800
18. Rosenkrantz, Abraham	115,800
19. Allen, Matthew	110,200
20. Pak, Young	109,200
21. Miller, Jim	106,700
22. Greenstein, Barry	106,600

23.	Harrington, Dan	106,100
24.	Shulman, Jeff	104,400
25.	Strzemp, John	103,400
26.	MONEYMAKER, CHRIS	100,900
27.	Benvenitsi, Tomer	94,800
28.	Lester, Jason	93,800
29.	Zeidman, Cory	92,600
30.	Inashima, John	91,300

PLAYERS REMAINING: 111

6.
DAY THREE

Chips become ammunition, and you're
going to war. If you've got a lot of bullets,
you're going to win the war.

—Johnny Chan,
world champion poker player

Another noon start, and this time I nearly managed to make it to my
table on time. Actually, I got pretty damn close. I made it to the main
floor with a couple minutes to spare, but then I couldn't find my
table. The tables were numbered and set out in loose chronological
order, but I roamed the floor a couple times and couldn't find Table
71, where I had been assigned. I thought, Well, where the hell is my
table? I checked the sheets again, to see if maybe I'd misread it, but
there it was: 71. Then I looked around for Johnny Chan and Howard
Lederer, two guys who are always easy to spot in a poker room for all
the activity they seem to generate, but I couldn't spot them either.
Next I thought maybe I'd missed something. I did another pass or
two around the room and still couldn't find my assigned table, so I
pulled over one of the tournament organizers and asked for help.

"Table Seventy-one," this guy said. "No wonder you can't find
it. That's the TV table."

I thought, Damn. The TV table? It was bad enough I'd been up
half the night, worried I was going to make a fool of myself in front

of Howard Lederer and Johnny Chan and Paul Darden and the other great players at my table, but now I'd have to worry about making a fool out of myself in front of a national television audience as well—and the bigger crowds that seemed to form around these headline players. Just my luck. It was like finding out that a camera crew was set up in your bathroom while a small crowd huddled in the shower watching your every move.

The TV table was over to the side of the main room, cordoned off from the other tables by its own railing. Each day, as players were knocked out and there were fewer and fewer tables, the area around the TV table became bigger and bigger. There was the same overall amount of poker real estate on the main floor, but the area around the tables kept expanding, with more and more room for the gallery. With all this attrition, the TV table went from sideshow to center stage. Even the outer tables became more prominent, given all this extra room the tournament organizers had to work with and the extra spectators they now had to manage. Players who had been eliminated from the tournament tended to stay and watch the later-round action, friends and family of the "surviving" players tended to come into town to root on their loved ones, and fans tended to come out in greater numbers as the intensity of the action increased over the final days. All of which made the idea of sitting in front of a small crowd, and a small television crew, about as intimidating as anything I'd faced so far in the tournament. Realize, the tables were randomly assigned, but tournament organizers and a production team from ESPN decided which of those random tables had the kind of firepower and star power they wanted to feature for that day of play—and here it was confirmed for me that this was probably the toughest table I could have drawn in the remaining field.

Believe me, the producers didn't target this table to track the fortuitously named accountant from Tennessee, playing in his first-ever poker tournament. I wasn't exactly the main storyline they were following. If I played my cards right—how's that for an appropriate expression?—I just might emerge as one of the stories of this World Series, but for now I was just another Internet hopeful, just some amateur playing over his head and under everybody else's radar.

An ESPN production assistant took me aside and told me the drill. There were tiny lipstick cameras built into the TV table at each seat position. The players were meant to look at their hole cards in such a way that the lipstick camera could pick them up. He had me practice it a couple times, to ensure that the cameras could "read" my cards and that I could still protect them to my own satisfaction. The assistant and an ESPN producer type assured me that no one else could see my cards except for one or two folks in the control room, which was located behind a curtain at the far side of the room. I was a little uncomfortable showing my cards like that, despite their assurances, but I didn't think I was in any kind of position to say anything about it. I mean, who the hell was I to complain about a lipstick camera?

As unhappy as I was to see Johnny Chan, Howard Lederer, Paul Darden, and some of these other big-time players at the table, that's how tickled they probably were to see me. I was a sight for sore eyes and short stacks. I may have been among the chip leaders, but I was still a green rookie as far as they were concerned. An Internet player. Hell, the white Poker Stars shirt I was wearing on this third day of play might as well have said FISH in big letters across the front, for the way I was advertising myself as an easy mark.

I knew, first sign of weakness, these guys would be all over me. They were the sharks, and I was chum.

First hand of the day set the tone—and for the time being anyway, the killer instincts at the table were put off my scent. Paul Darden, wearing his own pair of cool shades, drew a suited ace-queen and pushed all in, from a 36,000-chip position. The way he played it, it was an effortless call; he moved in easily, as if he had no choice, as if the cards had determined his action.

Howard Lederer, wearing a brown plaid shirt and looking every inch his "Professor" nickname, immediately called from his far stronger 204,800-chip position, showing a suited ace-nine.

Two strong hands. Two big bets. One big reshuffling of power at our table, no matter what the outcome.

I sat back and thought, Okay, this is going to get pretty interesting pretty quick. And then I thought that as long as I didn't do anything to contribute to "interesting," I'd be all right.

The flop came down ten-jack-queen, with two diamonds matching Paul Darden's suited opening hand, giving him a straight draw and a flush draw and almost every reason to think the hand would be his.

The turn was a six of diamonds, giving Darden the flush, leaving Lederer dead on the river, and launching Darden on a momentum run that would last for the next hour or so. On the very next hand, just to give you an idea what momentum can do at a tournament poker table, Darden drew pocket queens to Lederer's pocket tens—two more strong hands, to the same two strong players—and when Darden raised 40,000, Lederer was compelled to lay down his cards. It almost didn't matter what he was holding; he couldn't let the same player beat the crap out of him two hands in a row, first two hands of the day. Pocket tens is a damn strong hand, but I guess Howard Lederer didn't think it was damn strong enough at just this point in the tournament.

My strategy, at this Murderer's Row of a table, was to hang back until the cards forced me to play a hand. After he'd beaten up on me the night before, I wanted to steer clear of Johnny Chan and give myself time to study him close, see if there was anything I could pick up from a sideline position instead of getting mixed up with him on anything that was only marginally playable. I also wanted to get a good read on Howard Lederer, one of the game's great minds, and I didn't want to give either one of these guys—or anyone else at the table, for that matter—an opportunity to get a good read on me until I had some kind of hand. I didn't know enough about Paul Darden to worry about him, although from the way he ran the table early on, he was someone who deserved my serious attention.

I was in the one seat; Chan was in the three; Lederer was in the seven; and Darden was in the nine seat, immediately to my right. I was fat in the middle of a high-stakes, high-powered sandwich, so there was every reason to play with extreme caution. This was made clear almost every time someone thought to draw one of these players into a hand. Take Brian Haveson, an experienced player who was sitting between me and Chan in the two seat. Haveson had been CEO of NutriSystem. He had staked himself to a fairly impressive run in a couple tournaments, and he certainly had the bankroll to play with some of the game's true high rollers. When he turned up an ace-king, he figured he had to make a move. Some players wait weeks to catch an opening hand like that, and Haveson had to come out strong behind it. He made a big opening bet—15,000, which was about four or five times higher than the standard opening bet had been at our table up until this point.

Darden called with a four-five of clubs.

The flop was jack-queen-king, giving Haveson high pair on the board with an ace kicker and Darden a five-high club draw. It was Haveson's hand to play, and by the odds it was Haveson's hand to win, so he confidently pushed all in, adding about 30,000 in chips to the pot.

Now, Darden had a much stronger chip position and all kinds of momentum, but other than that he had no real reason to call the bet. I don't care how you're playing or what your strategy is—you don't risk that many chips on a flush draw unless you're on an all-out bluff, only here Haveson had already bought his way to the river with his all-in bet. The only thing Darden could do at this point was hope to win the hand outright, and the odds of that happening were just about totally against. If it was me, I don't think I would have been anywhere near that hand in that kind of pot, but Darden was all over it. With nothing. He even said as much as he made the call, but he made it anyway, and I wondered for about the millionth time that day how I'd ever make it past this table. How could I ever hope to match up against guys who were willing to risk so much on so little? Guys who had nothing to lose, to my everything to gain?

Haveson must have been wondering his version of the same. He couldn't believe that Darden would call with just a draw, especially on a six-figure pot, and he looked about ready to bust when the dealer flipped over the queen of clubs on the turn, giving Darden his flush and knocking Haveson from the tournament. I set out the hand here for the way it signals how quickly things changed as we moved toward these later rounds. You could have been on a strong, days-long run, playing with painstaking precision, only to lose everything in a flash, and here Brian Haveson went from thinking he might last out yet another day to kicking himself for thinking he could go head-to-head with just a lousy pair of kings.

There is no justice in poker—a simple fact, hardwired into the head of every serious player—and hands like this one prove the point and keep us up nights and leave us reaching for our backs to see if someone's stickered a KICK ME sign to our shirts.

The two seat was filled a couple hands later by a player named Kenna James, who very quickly tangled with Howard Lederer on a hand that wound up getting significant play on ESPN's World Series broadcast when it was finally shown a few months after the tournament.

Howard Lederer was one of the all-time masters of the piercing stare-down. He's a clean-cut, well-pressed guy who doesn't go in for the shades and ball caps and quirky props that are pretty much standard issue at these tournaments. No unlit cigars or ancient oranges or pictures of his wife or his kids or his dog. With Lederer it's a what-you-see-is-what-you-get kind of deal, and his only gimmick was the way he studied an opponent. Really, he was famous for how he could read the other players at the table, almost turned it into an art form, and when you went up against him for the first time, his reputation was about as intimidating as his actual abilities. Kenna James, after throwing in a big bet to support a hand of pocket queens, didn't want to give Lederer the slightest advantage, so what did he do? He pulled the collar of his jacket over his head, like a turtle, and zipped himself inside. Got a big laugh from everyone at our table—even from Lederer, who continued to stare this upstart down in a determined effort to put him on a hand.

Lederer, we all learned later, after the ESPN footage had been edited and produced, was sitting with pocket sixes—a hand he very much wanted to play, but only if he could get some sort of read on Kenna James. It really was a funny scene, especially because James had just joined our table and the sight of his jacket zipped over his head was our first impression, but my laughter was a little uneasy. Everyone, I think, was a little uneasy.

James couldn't see it, but Lederer continued to stare. For a full minute, which is a long time to stare down a jacket. James was giving off nothing, but Lederer would not shift his gaze or play his cards, and in that longest time, I got to thinking, There's just no way I'm betting into this guy unless I've got a killer hand.

After another minute or so, Lederer told James that it was okay for him to come out, that he was going to lay this hand down, and all the other players shared a good, nervous laugh and a huge sigh of relief that it hadn't been their chips on the line.

It was in this kind of tension-filled atmosphere that I made the bonehead move of the tournament—which, to my eternal discredit, quickly made its way onto ESPN's highlight reel, where it has been replayed over and over and over and then a couple dozen times more, forever branding me as an inexperienced Internet fish. Here's what happened: I was on the big blind, and I threw in my chips without even thinking about it, like a reflex. I didn't even bother to look at my cards, because I'd gotten it into my head that it can look pretty cool and intimidating when you come up against a player with the kind of patience to keep from checking his hand until the action comes around to him. Sometimes I looked as soon as the cards were dealt, and sometimes I didn't, and when I was on one of the blinds, I usually let the cards lie until the call came back around to me, but I was always mindful of how the not-looking would be perceived by the other players at the table. Here I guess I wanted everyone to think I was calm and confident and the picture of poker cool, so I left my cards facedown and watched the action run its way around the table.

And it zipped around pretty quick. It usually does when the blinds get steep. Kenna James, sitting to my left in early position—actually, "under the gun," first to act just after the big blind—threw in his cards. Johnny Chan, sitting to James's left, was holding king-jack and raised 4,000, chewing on a red swizzle stick as he counted out his chips. (His orange sat balanced on an empty glass that was keeping his chips company.) Everyone else folded around to Lederer, who raised 12,000 with an ace-queen. Paul Darden quickly folded, which placed the action back at me—only I didn't realize I was still in the hand. I was so intent on staring down Lederer and Chan, on finding some flaw or hole or tell that thousands of other players had somehow missed, that everything else fell away. We were about four hours into the day's action at this point, heading into a break, and I still hadn't managed to pick up a damn thing on either one of these guys. Man, there was nothing to read!

I put Chan, in early position, on a strong opening hand. When you're betting early like that, you tend not to bet big unless you have the cards in support. Lederer, one seat off the button, betting late in this hand, didn't need to have the best cards in the world to make them hold up. He had a chance to see what everyone else was going to do, and he figured at this late point he'd be going head-to-head with Chan, the only player betting ahead of him. Still, with his 12,000-chip raise, I put him on a strong hand, too. And that's where I got stuck. Looking at Chan, trying to figure out what the hell he was up to. Looking at Lederer, trying to figure out what the hell *he* was doing. And back and forth between the two for over a minute. That's a long time to be staring down your opponents when they're waiting on you to make a call. It's no time at all when you're out of the hand and looking on, waiting for the cards to play out and the dealer to move to the next hand. But when everyone else is looking to you for some kind of action, and you're stuck looking at them for some kind of tell, it's one giant stalemate. Chan had a pair of dark shades on, so I couldn't see his eyes. I knew he was looking at me, but I couldn't see his eyes. Lederer kept his eyes fixed on me, too, and as I sat there, now going on two minutes, I briefly wondered why the two of them weren't staring down each other. What the hell were they doing, looking at *me*? I actually thought about this and figured they probably had such a history, sitting across the table from each other at countless tournaments, that there was no need to waste time on each other when there was new meat at the table. And so they fixed on me.

I kept staring and concentrating and staring and concentrating. I was determined to pick something up. And as I stared and concentrated, the two of them stared and concentrated back. There were about eight tables of action on the other side of the TV rail, and there was more of a purr than a buzz about the room. Not exactly pin-drop quiet, but not a whole lot of commotion either. People were just going about their business, and so was I, desperate to pick up some kind of read on these two poker legends. It went on like this for almost three minutes, a helluva long time when you're sitting at a poker table waiting for someone to make a call. I didn't notice the time, but Chan and Lederer certainly did. And the other players at the table? They must have thought we'd see dinner before we'd see the flop. Chan and Lederer were probably thinking I was lost in strategy or trying to psych them off their hands. Hell, I've got no idea what they were thinking, but I'm pretty sure they assumed I knew what I was doing and that I must be doing *something*.

And then, finally, Chan broke. He nodded in my direction and said, "You know it's up to you, right?"

Well, I just turned six or seven shades of red, right there on that one seat. I'd completely forgotten I had a hand to play. Can you imagine how lame I must have felt? Remember, I was the big blind, so I was still in the hand, and here I'd been thinking I'd mucked my cards three minutes earlier and that I was just a spectator at this weird, inexplicable showdown between Johnny Chan and Howard Lederer. And all the time everyone else was waiting on *me* to make my call. I wanted to crawl under the table and die.

I pushed my cards across the table and apologized—profusely, sheepishly—and mumbled something about how I'd completely forgotten I was still in the hand. I tried to laugh it off, along with everyone else, but underneath I wasn't laughing. No, sir. Really, I'd never been so embarrassed—and for a beat or two in there, I gave some real thought to tanking the very next hand, just so I could get out of that room and find someplace to hide and call it a tournament. But the other guys at the table were good about their ribbing. Oh, make no mistake, they stuck it to me pretty fierce, but there was nothing mean-spirited about it. They all had a much-needed laugh, and it certainly sucked some of the tension from the table, and I managed to recover without looking like too much of an ass. I got razzed for a couple hands, is all. *Hey, Moneymaker. You in this hand or what?* That sort of thing. But it was all in good fun—good fun at my expense, mind you, but good fun just the same.

Looking back, I sometimes think my fool move went a long way toward setting me up for the rest of the tournament. I wouldn't recommend it as a kind of strategy, but it worked for me. I started to relax, just after that hand. All along I'd been thinking I was playing for pride—and now that pride was not an option, I let everything hang out. These big-time players at the table now had no reason to think I had the first idea what I was doing, so I fell somewhere between a fish and a wild card in their estimation, and I figured the only way to redeem myself was to play superaggressive from here forward. That had been my strategy for long stretches of the second day of the tournament, and it had served me well, and here I'd gotten bogged down in such a conservative, tentative game that I couldn't even keep track of my own call.

A couple hands later, I caught pocket aces and figured I'd take my not-so-new strategy for a test drive. I was in fairly early position, and a pair of aces was the highest opening Hold 'Em hand, so I made a 4,500 raise—a pretty moderate raise for that stage in the tournament. I hadn't played a whole lot of hands and didn't want to make so much noise with my opening bet that I scared off anyone else who was thinking of betting. It's tough to misplay pocket aces, but in retrospect I don't think I played the hand all that well, even though, when I watched it back on the edited ESPN coverage, the commentators seemed to think I did okay.

The action folded around to Howard Lederer in the big blind, who was dealt an ace-king, which also happens to be one of the top opening Hold 'Em hands in the deck, short of a high pocket pair. He raised 10,000.

I called. I didn't know it at the time, of course, but I had the advantage over Lederer before the flop. I might have reraised, but I worried if I pushed too hard before the flop, I'd push Lederer off the hand, so I made the conservative move.

The flop came down six-three-eight—no help to me, and most likely no real help to Lederer, unless he'd flopped a set.

Whatever he was holding, he must have liked his cards, because he threw another 25,000 in chips into the pot.

Whatever he was holding, I must have liked my cards a whole lot more, because I pushed all in.

Lederer had me about two to one in chips at this point, and he was sitting on a kick-butt hand of his own, so it was a bold, reckless move on my part, and it could have cost me the tournament. If I could take it back, I would have called, or made a small raise, but I guess I was still somewhat intimidated by Lederer's reputation. I was playing scared and naively thinking that the thing to do was scare the big gun off the hand.

Lederer thought about it for a good long while. I tried to match him stare for stare, behind my Oakleys, tried to make my face blank, to sit stock-still. I was afraid to breathe, thinking it might give something away. And, I'm sure, he was afraid to lay down an ace-king to a rookie who couldn't even remember whether or not he was still in a hand.

After a minute or so, Lederer pushed his cards across the table and folded his hand, and as I raked in the pot, I allowed myself a small smile. "I can breathe again," I said, after an exaggerated sigh.

I never knew what he was holding until I caught the action on ESPN some months later, and after that hand was shown, I thought, How about that, Money? You pushed Howard Lederer off an ace-king hand. I'd had him beat to that point in the hand, but I know how tough it is to lay down that kind of hand, so it really was a giant move for me.

I pushed Paul Darden off a six-seven on the very next hand, with a pair of Threes.

Darden opened with a 3,000-chip bet, and I immediately called.

We both checked after an ace-king-four flop.

The turn card was a ten, and Darden threw down a big bet.

I raised.

Darden folded. He'd just seen Howard Lederer lay down to me on an all-in bet, and Darden wasn't about to throw more money at the hot hand. Whatever momentum he had enjoyed early on at this table, it now appeared to have shifted to me. And I didn't mind the turnabout one bit.

Johnny Chan, meanwhile, was struggling. He's the kind of player that remains a factor with just one chip, but his stack had taken a slow pounding, and some of the stronger players at the table had begun to pick on him—at least insofar as anyone is ever able to pick on Johnny Chan. All session long, it seemed, he couldn't catch any cards, and when he did, he tried to make them count. He pushed me off a suited ace-three, with a 10,500-chip bet after the flop that I couldn't justify. He'd picked up a jack on the flop to make a pair and figured that was enough to make his hand—and in this case, against a starstruck nobody like me, it apparently was. I folded.

He pushed Howard Lederer off pocket eights just a few hands later, with an all-in bet after a three-seven-seven flop. Chan was holding ace-three, giving Lederer the stronger hand, but he pushed his last 29,400 in chips across the table and went for it. Much as he would have liked to have taken down "The Orient Express," and opened up the table for an end-of-session run, Lederer couldn't pull the trigger on the call and risk making Chan that much stronger. The call would have been nothing, from Lederer's comfortable chip position, but it would have been everything to Chan, who was really up against it—and sometimes, even in a head-to-head showdown, you have to think beyond the hand you're currently playing.

Just before our third break of the day, at about six-thirty, I had a chance to chase Johnny Chan from the tournament, and I grabbed at it. I was on the button. Chan was on the big blind. I raised 8,000 on a hand of eight of hearts–ace of hearts. It was a decent, nothing-special hand, but no one else seemed to want to play, and I couldn't see letting Chan add another blind to his dwindling stack without even a challenge. The break was announced, and all around the room, players had begun to step away from the table once they'd folded.

Chan called, making it a truly dramatic confrontation. No one was left at the table but the two of us, the rookie and the master.

The flop was ace of diamonds–three of hearts–four of hearts, giving me high pair on the board and a nut flush draw.

Chan checked after the flop.

I bet 4,500.

Chan check-raised, another 15,000.

I thought, Oh, crap. I figured I had him on this hand, and I knew I had him in chips, and I didn't like that he was trying to muscle me around. I didn't like what it said about his cards. When I flopped that ace, I was pretty comfortable that I was in the lead. Then, when he checked, I knew I was in the lead. Now, after he had come over the top on me like that, I put him on a high pocket pair at best. Or, more likely, on an ace-queen, ace-jack. I was liking my cards a lot with this flop, which had given me a whole mess of outs, but I wasn't liking Chan's action, so I considered my options. I could call and see where we were after the turn, but I didn't want to call. I wanted Chan to call with his chips, to force him to make the decision. I could reraise a modest amount and bet back into him, although I didn't think at this point that there was any way I could push Chan off the pot. About the only thing I couldn't do was fold. It wasn't a slam dunk hand by any stretch, but I was playing these cards—no matter what.

If I lost the hand, I lost the hand, but I didn't want to get out-played by the great Johnny Chan.

So what did I do? I moved all in. It wasn't really much of a call, from a tactical perspective. I had Chan about four to one in chips, so I wasn't risking that much behind a pretty strong hand. Unlike Howard Lederer, I didn't really care about making Chan healthy if he managed to come away with the pot. I suppose if I had been an experienced tournament player, I would have taken this last into account, but I couldn't see past my own stack. Anyway, a part of me just assumed that Chan was always healthy, long as he was still at the table. I wasn't thinking long term or big picture. I just wanted this pot, and if I could take down Johnny Chan along with it, then that would be gravy.

There was a small whir of excitement with my all-in bet, especially coming from the TV table. Most times when a former champion or a marquee-type player is pushed all in, players at other tables are able to pick up what's going on. They have a kind of sixth sense, whenever one of the big guns is in danger of falling. Plus, the news seems to run through the crowd like electricity—or like one of those childhood games of Telephone we all used to play. In this instance the small whir was amplified somewhat by the fact that a lot of the remaining players were already milling about the main room, at the front end of their break. They weren't tethered to their own tables. And so, as Chan considered his next move, a crowd began to gather around our table. The seats were all empty, but the rail was soon two or three deep.

Chan chomped on his swizzle stick and sniffed his orange and stared me down. And then, with his back to the wall, he threw up his hands and said, "All right." He pushed in his chips to call the bet, in what was probably the biggest what-the-hell bet I'd seen in my limited tournament experience.

Hey, this kid Moneymaker is pushing Chan all in over at the TV table.

That game of Telephone kicked itself up a notch, and there was a minicrush at the rail surrounding our table.

Chan's all in.

The buzz was in the air, and all around, and soon enough the TV table was rimmed by players and hangers-on, anxious to be let in on the fuss.

"I need a heart, dealer," I said, soon as Johnny Chan made the call. I stood and stepped back from the table as I showed my cards.

Chan heard me call out for hearts and knew he was screwed. He turned over king of hearts–five of hearts, a slightly lesser version of the same hand I'd been holding. He was looking at the same heart draw that I was looking at, but my ace had his king all kinds of beat. Plus, I'd managed to link up the high pair on the flop, so my hand was looking pretty good at that point—and Chan's chances pretty grim. He had two chances at an inside-straight draw, but the odds were far in my favor. All along, he must have thought he had tons of outs, and he did, but my hearts in the hole wiped out his flush draw, so he needed kings on the turn *and* the river, or a deuce, to fill out his straight.

"Oh," he said, "I'm in bad shape."

Oh, he was.

I felt bad about it, for about a heartbeat. After all, this was *Johnny Chan*. The man was like a poker god, and I hated like hell that it fell to me to bring him down even as I loved the hell out of it, if that makes any sense. It was cool and not cool, sweet and bittersweet, the stuff of my dreams and the stuff of my disillusions, all bundled together, all at once.

"Put a deuce up there," Chan said to the dealer, not giving up without a fight.

"No deuce!" I shouted back. "No deuce!"

The turn card was a nine of hearts—no deuce!—which gave me the flush, and the hand, and every reason to cheer. I let out a little rebel yell, but then I checked myself. I didn't want to rub this guy's nose in it. He deserved better than that. He was Johnny Chan, "The Orient Express," and I was just some pissant accountant on a wild adventure. Yeah, I had every reason to celebrate, but I didn't think that was the way to play it, so I played it down. All these people had spilled from their tables to watch this showdown. It was the last hand of the session, so all eyes were on me and Chan, and I didn't want to come off as some blowhard newbie bent out of shape on a winning turn card. So I caught myself and caught my breath, and I silently strode over to Chan to shake his hand.

"Nice hand," he said.

"Thanks," I said.

And that was that.

Course, inside I was seriously pumped, and I wanted desperately to seek out my buddy Bruce across the room and whoop it up some. It wouldn't do, and it wasn't cool, but I'd just knocked out Johnny Chan! It was tough to choke down those emotions, let me tell you. There's that great scene in *Rounders* where Matt Damon puts a move on Chan and then his buddy is all over him, telling him, "You took out Chan! You took out Chan!" It's a great scene and a great line, and here I was, living it for real. That's where my head was, at just that moment, and as I left the table and made for the bathroom, I got back-slaps and congratulations and high fives, with folks saying essentially the same thing: *You took out Chan! You took out Chan!* It was a weird, almost surreal case of life imitating art, and sure enough when I finally hooked up with Bruce, that was the first thing out of his mouth: "You took out Chan!"

(And, also sure enough, I'll hear that line in airports and hotel lobbies and casinos . . . probably for the rest of my life.)

Yes, I took out Chan, and I thought, Well, if this is it for me—if this is as good as it gets and I somehow manage to blow my chips and crash and burn and fall out of the money—at least I'll have this. I might not win a dime, but at least I won't go home empty-handed. At least I'll have a story.

Months later, when the ESPN footage finally came on television, the announcer, Norman Chad, compared my showdown with Chan to Buster Douglas knocking out Mike Tyson, and that's about how it was. For me, anyway, that's about how it was, and I wasn't about to question it, or mess with it, or set it aside.

As it happened, this third day of play was scheduled to be an abbreviated session. After two marathon days, when the action stretched until midnight and beyond, we were set to break for the night at dinner, to give the still-standing players a chance to get some sleep before making their final push. Four two-hour sessions, to winnow the field from the 111 players we had going in to to-day's play to the 45 that would open the action tomorrow. The key here is that there was prize money to be paid out, beginning with the sixty-third-place finisher, so tournament organizers now had to determine precisely what time each player was chased from the tournament in order to start awarding prize money to their in-the-money finishers. One way they did this was to run each table on the same clock, with dealers at the few remaining tables coordinating their hands to prevent up-against-it players from slow-playing their way into prize money. It used to be that players facing elimination could nurse their hands and draw out their calls, waiting on someone else to get eliminated a beat or two before them, but the synchronized clock took care of that strategy. It was like the tournament version of those last-longer bets they had going at some of the satellite tables earlier in the week, but they had to be played out on a level field.

The low-end prize money would have been a disappointment to any of these high-end players, but it would have been a boon to me. The bottom nine in-the-money places—sixty-third through fifty-fifth—paid $15,000, nearly double what I had hoped to collect from that fourth-place Poker Stars prize just a few weeks earlier, and as we got down to about sixty-five or seventy players left, I silently congratulated myself. In-the-money, for me, was huge; $15,000, for me, was huge. Even with the 45 percent stake I'd have to pay out to my dad and my buddies for backing me, it was huge. Remember, my goal had been to last out that first day, and once I'd accomplished that, I went gunning for the second day. Now, on the third day, I was determined to take home at least *some* prize money— to pay down my credit cards and get us close to whole at last—but at the same time, there was a part of me that would have been disappointed, too. All of a sudden, I was close enough to the final table to where *that* had now become the target. The prize money was fine, and very much needed, but I had such a strong stack at this point that it was also a given. I'd finish in the money. I'd have to.

One by one, leading up to the dinner break on the third day, the big-name players began to fall. Barry Greenstein, the chip leader after the first day of play, finished in forty-ninth place just before the end of the final session of the day, earning $20,000. Annie Duke, Lederer's sister and the last surviving woman in the tournament, hung on for another couple hands but was finally put out in forty-seventh place, also earning $20,000, and she was quickly followed by a player named Bui Jules, who grabbed another $20,000 prize.

That left us with forty-five players to begin the fourth day of play—nine tables, with a payout to the forty-fifth- to thirty-seventh-place finishers of $25,000.

The best I could hope for was now the worst I could do—

$25,000—and I spilled out of the Horseshoe that night like I was on top of the world.

Twenty-five thousand dollars! Man, that was everything for Kelly and me. A brand-new baby we couldn't afford. A brand-new house we couldn't afford. Double-digit credit-card and gambling debts we couldn't afford. And now I was looking at getting us out from under. At long last. All on the back of a good run of cards. And, to top it off, I had taken out Johnny Chan!

Bruce and I decided to have a couple cocktails to celebrate and then head back to Binion's for some more poker. We found a $5/$10 pot-limit table and sat ourselves down, wanting to let off some steam. The poker room at Binion's is always packed, at every hour of the day, but I didn't recognize any of the players who were still alive in the World Series tournament. I guess most of those guys were sick of playing, or wanting to keep fresh for the next day of play, but I can play poker any old time. I can go thirty-six hours straight, no problem, and here I just wanted to sit down with Bruce and play, get my mind off the tournament. Unwind. Trouble was, there was no unwinding—not for me, not in this room. I couldn't set foot in that poker room without being recognized by all the poker groupies who were in town for the tournament. Players who'd been eliminated or who had played in one of the preliminary events. Guys with weekend or neighborhood games who happened to be in town and had been taking in some of the action. Folks knew my name. They knew my chip count. They knew I'd taken out Johnny Chan. And every last person I met had a couple words of advice: *Be aggressive. Hang back and pick your spots. Play your game. Be patient. Mix things up, every few hands.*

Some of it was good advice. Some of it was predictable cliché. And I didn't listen to any of it, because I was off in my own head, playing pot-limit with my good buddy Bruce, taking it all in, looking forward to tomorrow, and not wanting this day to end.

CHIP LEADERS: CLOSE OF PLAY, DAY THREE ♥ ♣ ♠ ♦

Player	Chip Count
1. Fitoussi, Bruno	671,500
2. Boyd, Dutch	491,500
3. Nguyen, Scotty	428,500
4. Hellmuth, Phil	362,000
5. Watkins, Bryan	360,500
6. MONEYMAKER, CHRIS	357,000
7. Farha, Sam	354,000
8. Singer, David	334,000
9. Shulman, Jeff	327,500
10. Hoang, Chuc	264,500
11. Lester, Jason	261,500
12. Nguyen, Minh	251,500
13. Vahedi, Amir	237,500
14. Deeb, Kassam Ibrahim	232,000
15. Thorson, Olof	227,000
16. Brenes, Humberto	227,000
17. Lederer, Howard	224,500
18. Harrington, Dan	176,500
19. Luske, Marcel	174,500
20. Grigorian, Chris	174,000

PLAYERS REMAINING: 45

7.
DAY FOUR

Poker is a lot like sex. Everyone thinks
they're the best, but most people don't
know what they're doing.

> —Dutch Boyd, poker player

Every table is dangerous at this late stage of the tournament, every seat assignment shot through with all kinds of worry, every opponent the one to knock you out or play into your hand. For the start of the fourth day of play, I drew a tough seat alongside chip leader Bruno Fitoussi, Jason Lester, Humberto Brenes, Dennis Waterman, and Jim Miller, the tournament director. Big-time players all—with big-time chip stacks to match. Frankly, there were "tougher" tables (imagine drawing a seat next to Phil Ivey, Scotty Nguyen, Jeff Shulman, Men "The Master" Nguyen, and Howard Lederer, as happened to Olof Thorson, the only other Poker Stars player still alive in the tournament), but the experienced hands at my table were more than formidable enough for me, and I studied the sheets before sitting down and longed for that kinder, gentler table where I'd opened the tournament.

Jeez, I thought, had it been three full days already? Had I made it this far? And the big question: Would I make it through another day? That had always been the realistic goal, to last out each day, and if I managed to do so one more time, I'd reach the Final Table—poker's equivalent of the Final Four. That was really the ultimate for me. I didn't dare think of winning the whole damn thing—not just yet. But the Final Table was definitely within reach. I'd score me a cool Final Table jacket, get my name up on a cool plaque, and be forever immortalized among the couple dozen mortals who pay attention to such things. As important, I'd guarantee myself considerable prize money—even the ninth-place finisher, the first guy chased from the Final Table, was looking at a payout of $120,000.

Bruno Fitoussi controlled most of our action for the first hour or so, which we might have predicted given his commanding position—671,500 in chips, nearly 200,000 more than his next-closest competitor, Dutch Boyd, at 491,500. Fitoussi had me almost two to one in chips at the start of play, and he had everyone else three to one or better, and that kind of strength really determines a lot of the betting in these later rounds, when folks tend to play a little tighter, when each hand seems to matter a little more than the hand before. He also had such a far-reaching reputation among high-stakes poker players that even I knew who he was. Fitoussi was only a few years older than me, but he was one of the owners of Aviation Club de France, a really nice poker room in Paris. I'd actually played there a couple times when I was in graduate school, back when I didn't know the first thing about poker but was determined to learn on a student's budget, which in my case no longer had any room in it for serious gambling. I was staying about two blocks from the club, and I didn't know anybody in town, and there wasn't a whole lot to do at night, so I wandered in, thinking my nothing budget could manage a couple hands. Of course I was turned away. There was a strict dress code, and my jeans and T-shirt didn't quite cut it, so I went out the next day and got fitted for a suit—a nice suit, too, as I recall. Like I said, I was pretty committed to learning the game, and I figured the best way to learn was to watch the best players I could find and to look damn good doing it. I pretty much lost my shirt (*and* my brand-new suit, as well), but I picked up a thing or two on the way out. They played all kinds of weird games over in Paris—five cards in your hand and five on the table, in one ring game I stumbled into—and I was totally outclassed, but I didn't mind being outclassed in such a classy joint.

So I felt pretty good about myself, sitting down in the four seat across from Bruno Fitoussi in the eight, thinking that this might be a big-time professional player, playing behind a big-time professional stack—but I'd played in his club, on his terms, and in my head that put us at about the same level. It leveled our stacks some. Don't misunderstand, the guy had me a whole lot better than two to one in experience, and I was still pinching myself over the fact that I had lasted to this fourth day of play, but I was trying to bring these players down in whatever ways I could. And, level playing field or not, I still planned to steer clear of him, also in whatever ways I could. For his part, Fitoussi played just about every hand, right out of the gate, raising big each time. I thought, Good night! And, Watch out! I wondered, How am I supposed to go up against *that*? Really, Fitoussi was all over the table, betting three times the big blind on nothing hands, sometimes more, and stealing blinds and punishing raises and pushing folks off their pots almost on a whim. After a while of this, I decided to try to match Bruno's bullying tactics. If anyone else had the kind of stack for that kind of game, it would be me, and if I meant to keep it and to add to it every few hands, I'd need to adopt a more proactive style of play. And that's just what happened. Fitoussi would raise, and I would reraise. Or *I* would raise, and *he* would reraise. Eventually one of us would blink, but after I jumped into the action, a good percentage of the first couple dozen pots went to one or the other of us. It was like a bizarre dance, with each of us trading off the lead.

Most of the second hour of play was stamped by this high-stacked back-and-forth I had going on with Bruno Fitoussi, until I finally caught a pair of pocket eights. Wasn't much, but it was the best hand I'd seen in the round thus far, and I wanted to see if I could make something happen, make some kind of run to the chip lead for our table. Humberto Brenes, the flamboyant Costa Rican who wore loud, colorful scarves and two pairs of glasses (one for seeing, one for hiding behind), was sitting to Fitoussi's left in the nine seat, on the button. I was in early position and made a small raise—about 15,000 in chips. Fitoussi thought to sit this one out and folded, and the call came to Brenes, who reraised me another 15,000 or so. Now, this guy was an excellent player, with a list of tournament wins and Final Table finishes that ran longer than one of his scarves, but he hadn't played a whole lot of hands so far at this table, and I didn't think he'd be willing to commit over 30,000 in chips on a nothing hand. Still, it wasn't a killer bet. He had a stack of about 150,000, so the move fell somewhere between conservative and aggressive, and I was caught weighing the fact of his playing the hand in the first place against the tentative way he was seeming to play it. Absolutely, it was something to consider, and the thing that struck me about the bet was how Brenes made it. He stood and stepped back from the table—something I'd seen him do the night before, heads up against Scotty Nguyen, on a nothing-special hand. Only other time I'd seen him do it, and he was on a draw, so here I put him on something like the same. Ace-jack, maybe. King-ten. Something like that. He was walking around scratching his face, sliding his spectacles low on his nose, and staring down at me from on top of them. He even sang a little bit, after the flop, and I thought, Okay, if these aren't a whole bunch of nervous tells, then I'm just a nervous rookie in over my head.

I called.

The flop: king-nine-deuce.

I checked.

Brenes—standing, singing, scratching, pacing—came back with another 30,000-chip bet. This from a guy who hadn't gotten up from his seat all day long, who had gone through some of these same motions the day before when Scotty Nguyen called him out on a hand he didn't really want to play. I didn't know it at the time, but Humberto Brenes was sitting with pocket aces, and here I was reading him like he'd caught a straight draw at best.

I was, more than likely, doomed. And I didn't have a clue.

Realize, pocket eights is not the strongest hand in the world, but it can be strong enough when you're playing heads up and the flop doesn't offer all that much. I had Brenes by about 150,000 in chips, and I considered our chip positions as I considered my response. If I called him, I'd still have to worry about my action after the turn card. I'd thought he might be holding an ace, and if the turn was another ace, I'd be in a real bind. If that happened, I could get outplayed. I didn't mind getting beat, but I didn't want to get outplayed. (Of course, I didn't put Brenes anywhere close to his pocket aces at this point, so I was getting seriously outplayed already.) If he moved all in after a favorable turn, I'd have to lay down, and I wasn't planning on laying down. Mine was the bigger stack, by a whole bunch, and I figured I'd have to use the fact that Brenes didn't want to be pushed out of the tournament to my advantage. I'd have to find some way to scare him off the hand, without leaving myself too vulnerable. Where the cards didn't help, the chips didn't hurt. If I made a small raise—say, to 50,000—Brenes might hang around just to see if he could catch something on a draw, so the *weight* of my response was critically important.

And so I pushed all in—thinking (hoping!) Brenes would lay down. Or thinking (hoping!) my eights would hold up.

Brenes watched me push my chips to the center of the table and his smile grew wide enough to accept mail. Then he called, and he waved his finger at me in a *tsk-tsk* gesture, like a grown-up catching a child with his hand in the cookie jar. Which is exactly what he had just done.

I knew I was in trouble, but when he turned over those aces, I thought I'd die. I thought I'd be down to about 150,000 in chips and scrambling to hold on instead of battling for the lead—and Brenes, smiling and dancing and singing and waving his finger at me, didn't help.

I stood and stepped back from the table myself, calling out for an eight. And, sure enough, an eight came on the turn. It was the most remarkable thing. I thought, How about that! I was standing and praying and trying to match this guy gesture for gesture, and an eight came along to bail me out. I jumped up and down and hugged a couple guys along the rail I didn't even know and threw my fist in the air like I'd just won the lottery—which in a way I had, because there wasn't a whole lot of skill in how I'd just played this hand. This was the luck of the draw, and I didn't mind the outcome even as I hated the hard road I'd taken to it.

Man, I was pumped! Frazzled, too, from thinking I'd botched things, but mostly pumped. And a little over the top about it, looking back. On the ESPN footage, you can see me almost punch this guy in the front row of the gallery, my arms were flailing about in excitement so wildly.

This celebration went on for just a few seconds, until I caught myself and realized that Brenes must have been distraught, to get put out of the tournament with cards like that. Pocket aces! So I walked over to him and held out my hand and apologized for my behavior—and for knocking him out.

He couldn't have been nicer about it. Really, Humberto Brenes was a real class act. World-class player. World-class good sport. Never won the World Series, but he'd made a lot of Final Tables.

"Hey," he said. "You know, it happens."

Yes, it does. All the time. Only it doesn't usually happen to me, so it took some getting used to. I'd been beat, made a devastatingly bad read, but the cards had smiled on me, and I let myself think that anytime you get outplayed and still come away with the pot, it's a good hand. It stays with you, and it even keeps you up nights, but it's still a good hand. At least you talk yourself into *believing* it's still a good hand. When Brenes stood up and walked around the table the day before, heads up against Scotty Nguyen, he had an ace-ten with nothing on the board, and I put his prancing around the same way as a tell. I thought he was bluffing. I had been at the table with him and Nguyen, and when I saw him make the same play on day four, the same gesture, I put him on the same kind of hand. No way did I put him on pocket aces. Hell, I didn't put him on a pair of pocket anything—just a couple high cards he was hoping to parlay into something bigger. So what did I do? I made a play at the pot, raised him all his chips. I did this on the sound theory that when you put a man to all his chips, it puts a lot of pressure on him, but when the man is sitting with pocket aces, it's not all that much pressure. I knew I was in trouble soon as Brenes called the bet. He did it with a song in his heart and in his every movement; the guy just reeked of joy, which I guess is how most players would have shown that kind of hand.

I ended up catching my card, but Humberto Brenes outplayed me on the hand, and much as I liked raking in all his chips, I hated that I'd been outplayed.

My father arrived at Binion's just as this hand with Brenes was playing out, and as he made his way through the gallery to our table, he heard all kinds of commotion. He didn't know what was going on. Most folks, a row or two behind the rail, didn't know what was going on. There's a big screen that dominates one side of the room, but there's no way to read the cards everyone is playing except to eavesdrop on the small talk and banter and fill in the blanks from the body language. A hand to the head usually meant someone got beat. A fist in the air usually meant that someone had done the beating. Two fists in the air . . . well, that was a serious beating. Best my father could figure from the buzz in the room was that the kid Moneymaker was all in against the Costa Rican with the two pairs of glasses, and he fairly raced to Bruce Peery's side, out of breath, wanting to know what he'd missed. For a beat or two, he'd thought maybe he'd flown all the way out from Knoxville just to have me out of the tournament before he could watch a single hand.

"Chris just got superlucky," Bruce said to my dad, not mincing words. "Guy had pocket aces, and Chris moved him all in with a pair of eights."

"And Chris took the hand?" my father wanted to know. He was still putting two and two together, still not clear what had happened.

"Caught another eight on the turn," Bruce said. "Got bailed out."

My father breathed a big sigh and allowed himself a small holler in relief. "Go, Money!" he shouted out, getting into the spirit of things. "Hey, Money!"

He caught my attention, flashed a giant smile, and then pumped his fist in a way that had me thinking it was genetic.

You know, once the World Series footage began airing on ESPN, I started hearing from all kinds of folks that I was the luckiest man they'd ever seen, that I was living some kind of charmed life during the run of the tournament, that the only reason I won was because the cards kept falling my way, and it always gnaws at me. One of the ESPN announcers, in analyzing this particular hand, said I'd been "walking through raindrops" for the entire tournament, and I don't think that's entirely fair. Clearly, I was lucky on this one hand, and I was lucky on a couple other big hands during the run of play, but every hand has some measure of luck in it. It's lucky to be dealt pocket aces in the first place (220–1, against) or to catch a flush draw from an opening hand that looked like nothing. It's lucky when your pocket threes hold up against two other players. Folks watching the edited version of the World Series on television, they see a couple dozen pivotal hands and think that was the extent of my tournament, but I played hundreds of hands that week at Binion's. Maybe a thousand, by conservative count, and most of those hands I played well. Some of them I played poorly. And every now and then, I found myself with a strong opening hand that I didn't play at all. Check this out: I drew ace-king four times in the tournament and folded preflop, so clearly it's not just about luck, and it's not just about following some predictable course and hoping your cards come home. It's about picking your spots and liking your chances and making the most of those chances. And, yeah, it's about getting lucky, and keeping yourself in position to get lucky, for as long as possible, as often as possible.

Another ace-king lay-down, this one postflop, came during this fourth day of play—against no less an opponent than Howard Lederer, back at the same table for another run at my stack. Another nine players had already been eliminated from the start of play, and we were down to four tables, and I had about 700,000 in chips—my high-water mark to that point. Lederer made a big raise, about 40,000, which I quickly called—because, when you've got the chips to back it up, you've got to play those ace-king hole cards. The flop was just rags—low cards that didn't do a single thing for me, nor (I was betting) for Lederer, but Lederer came back with another 40,000 raise, which I had to call. There was no help on the turn, but I figured I'd make a play for the pot. I'd thrown about 100,000 in chips into this one pot, and now I pushed in another 90,000, hoping to push Lederer off the hand in the bargain. But he pushed back—all in. And I was stuck. I'd committed almost 200,000 in chips at a time when I wasn't planning on getting mixed up in anything big, and here I was thinking about committing some 200,000 more. I thought about it, and I thought about it, and I thought about it, all the way to forever, until finally I folded.

Lederer didn't have to show me his cards, but he did: pocket queens. He had me. I'd made the right call, but he'd made the right play, and it ended up costing me a whole mess of chips.

Sometimes a winning run doesn't have near as much to do with luck as it does with muscle and position, and I was reminded of this again a short while later, after I was assigned a seat directly to Scotty Nguyen's right, where I was soon dealt a king-queen. I had almost 600,000 in chips, and he had just over 300,000, so I raised 75,000.

Nguyen called.

Three-eight-seven came on the flop—with two clubs on the board to link up with my king.

I bet another 75,000.

Nguyen raised me 75,000, and I thought, Oh, crap. One of the best players in the world is betting into me, big time. I thought, This sucks. I thought, I'm screwed. He'll be sitting on my bets and my blinds all damn day. Then I thought about laying down my hand, which was probably the prudent move, but I just couldn't do it. My gut told me I still had the stronger hand, else Nguyen would have done more than simply call my bet right out of the gate. Maybe he'd caught a pair on the flop, or maybe he was looking at the same flush draw that I was now looking at, but I'd have him there, too, unless he held the ace of clubs.

For whatever reason, by whatever logic, I thought I was in the lead on the hand, even though Scotty Nguyen didn't tell me a damn thing. By his actions, by his inactions—there was nothing to read, not that I could figure. I'd been watching this guy for the longest time, and he didn't give off any kind of signal, but my instincts kept telling me to push the hand. Either it was my instincts or it was just wishful thinking, but that was my one thought, to keep pushing the hand. I could have been totally wrong, and I'd already been totally wrong on another big hand, but that's what I did. I reraised another 75,000, and it did the trick. Nguyen laid down his hand, and as he did so, I quickly showed my cards to Dutch Boyd, a young gun of a player with a rakefree.com visor, a bad-boy repu-tation, and a serious stack of chips, who was sitting immediately to my right. I wanted him to know, in this passing way, that I'd just bluffed the great Scotty Nguyen—not to blow smoke up my own butt or to humiliate Nguyen but to give Dutch Boyd something to think about, if he was thinking about stealing some of my blinds. It was the kind of posturing move you don't get to make when you're playing online—normally, when you fold a hand online, you can show your cards to all the players at the table or to no one—but here I thought it would serve me well to show another young player like Boyd, who'd been up among the leaders all day long, that I wasn't some knee-jerk, by-the-book player. It was information I wanted him to have, in case we got mixed up in a hand before too long.

Which of course we did—but not just yet.

First, heading into the dinner break, there was an anxious

showdown with a player named Chuc Hoang, one of those strong, silent types who tended to stay away from the action unless he had something worth playing. It was probably about seven o'clock in the evening, and we were just into our fourth two-hour session of the day. We were now down to about thirty players, and I had been playing at the same table with Hoang for a couple hours. I don't think he got involved in more than a dozen hands in all that time. He struck me as a good player, but extremely conservative.

I was dealt ace-three of hearts.

I had position on Hoang, but he had made a strong raise, which I quickly called. No one else wanted in on the hand, so it was just the two of us, heads up, before the flop. I'd built my stack back up to about 700,000 after that tanked Lederer hand, and Hoang had about half that amount.

The flop was an eight-nine-ten—no hearts.

Hoang checked, which I took to be a sudden sign of weakness. It made no sense that he was checking, after betting strong into me on the first pass, and I couldn't think what he might have. It was an interesting flop, but only if you had the hole cards to make it interesting.

I checked, too, which I thought would at least buy me some time to consider the turn card and see what this guy might do next.

The turn was a six, after which Hoang bet 15,000—a weak bet at this late stage of the tournament and at this late stage in the hand. Really, it was a nothing bet, a spec, considering our two stacks and his much stronger opening bet before the flop, so I raised him 15,000. Also a nothing raise, but I wanted to push him on his own terms. And besides, I *had* nothing.

I had no idea what kind of hand to put this guy on, but I didn't think it was strong. I was pretty sure he didn't have a seven, because he'd only checked after the flop. Plus, the way this guy had been playing, he wouldn't have raised preflop with a seven, unless of course it was pocket sevens. It was possible he had a jack-something. Jack-ace. Jack-king. Jack-queen. Naturally, if he had that jack-queen, he'd have flopped a straight, and I was dead. But even these high cards, linked or not, didn't suggest such a soft opening bet.

This was the first time I'd gotten tangled up in a hand with Chuc Hoang, and one of the first hands I'd seen him play past the flop, so I had no real history on him. All I could go on were the couple leaps I'd allowed myself to make in figuring his mind-set. I was all over the place in my thinking, but never to where I considered folding, which was probably the smartest move I could have made. At least it would have been the safest move. For now, though, it was Hoang's call to make, and after an interminable wait, he reraised me another 15,000. I thought, Come on already, make a real bet! Or fold! Show some determination, one way or the other.

I reraised 100,000, thinking I'd make a play at the pot and at the same time get to see where this guy was with his hand. The move took me down to about 400,000 in chips. If he called, he'd be down to approximately 180,000. He thought about it for maybe a month. And then, for good measure, a little while longer. Finally, it looked like he was ready to make his move.

"I'm going to pay you off," he said softly—and this struck me then as possibly the worst words I could have heard.

Hoang was throwing in the towel on the hand without actually throwing in the towel on his hand, indicating that he thought I had the better of him but that he was so committed to the pot he was going to call me anyway.

I thought, Aw, jeez, I've got no outs. And, truly, I didn't. There wasn't a single card in that deck that would have made the slightest difference for me. Last I'd checked, nothing plus nothing still turned up nothing, and that's what I was looking at. There was no way I could win the hand outright, and I was about 100,000 chips past the point of no return.

The river was a jack—potentially all kinds of help to Hoang. Also, potentially, no help at all.

Hoang checked, which told me a bunch and at the same time not a whole lot. Told me he probably still hadn't caught a powerful hand, but there remained the possibility that he'd caught his straight and was trying to dupe me into thinking I still had a hand. A queen was key, and he probably thought I was sitting with one, or that I thought he was sitting with one—or hell, maybe he *was* actually sitting with one. I had no good idea at this point, but I didn't think he would risk me checking to the scare card on the river. Whatever that last jack may or may not have meant to the rest of his hand, I didn't think it was the card he was waiting on.

I was hoping he had put me on a straight, and I was trying to present that I'd caught my straight, and I was thinking the best case for him was a pocket pair of some kind that he might have played into a set with one of the community cards. Jacks, maybe, going back to my earlier hunch.

I thought about checking, but I didn't think there was any way I could win the hand. I had that ace for a kicker, but I didn't think it would come down to the kicker. The only move, really, was to smoke him out, so after some major deliberation, I pushed all in—hoping Hoang would crumble. That old saw about not throwing good money after bad rings true every damn time, but here I thought this last piece of good money might take the pot—because, after all, I still had some good money left to burn.

Once again Hoang thought about his next move. After the longest time, he said, "I guess you have the queen."

He hadn't folded just yet, so I was careful not to respond. He was about to, everyone could feel it, but so far it was just talk. I sat stone-faced behind my Oakley Straightjackets, the bill of my Poker Stars cap pulled low over my face, and underneath I was thinking those were about the best words I had heard all day. He put me on the queen, and he was toast.

He tossed his cards back toward the dealer soon enough, and I said, "No, sir. No queen." I was mock polite about it, with a kind of swagger to my voice, an edge. Then I threw my cards across the table, faceup, with a quick snap of the wrist, almost like I was lording it over this guy, that I had pushed him off his hand. I'd won the pot, but I hadn't put Hoang out, and my thinking here was that maybe if I strutted, I could put him on tilt a little bit. Get him pissed at himself, or at me, for misplaying his hand and misreading mine, leave him off his game for the next while.

Everyone else at the table kind of gasped when I showed my cards, which of course was the desired effect. No one could believe I'd throw so many chips at such a hard-core, flat-out bluff, and the common knowledge that I would could only help me from here on in. That's how I looked at it. No one could guess what I would do, for the rest of the tournament, which made this such an incredibly important hand. The field was thin enough by this point that word of this hand would run through the room like electricity, and I could only benefit from the buzz.

As it happened, this particular hand never made it to the edited ESPN footage—I don't think they had it on camera, is why—but it was the talk of the tournament leading up to the dinner break. And now, in retrospect, it stands out as perhaps my best play of the World Series. I played in bigger, more meaningful hands, and I won bigger, more meaningful pots, and I knocked out or wounded bigger, more meaningful opponents, but no other hand came close to this one for pure gamesmanship. No other hand got close to this one for balls and chops and bluster. I mean, this was poker. This was what the game was all about. This was why we played. Forget the luck of the draw, this was about having the stones to hang in against no luck whatsoever. This one hand did a whole lot of business for me, beyond the chips I was able to collect on the strength of it, and I look back on it now as an in-your-face reminder that if you never make a bluff at a pot, you're never going to win a damn thing. You can't always have the best hand. No, sir. You've got to find ways to win when you've got no hand at all, and here I'd found a way to win and was damn glad of it.

I asked Hoang later what he'd been holding, and he told me he had a seven, and I was damn glad about that, too. I never saw the seven, mind you, but I don't think he would have admitted to it if it weren't the case, and it made it all that much sweeter to know that I'd pushed him off a straight.

My dad and Bruce and now Dave Gamble, my other main "backer," were high-fiving each other behind the rail, and I was all bent out of shape with excitement, and none of us were too terribly shy about whooping it up in celebration. We had a real party going on in my corner of the gallery. Unlike the lucky knockout draw against Humberto Brenes, I didn't let myself worry if I was rubbing Chuc Hoang's nose in anything. He was a nice enough guy, I'm sure, and I could be a nice enough guy when the situation called for it, but here the situation didn't call for nice. Not yet. Chuc Hoang was still very much alive. I'd only weakened him with this hand, and we were at a point in the tournament where we had to kick our opponents when they were down. That's how it goes when you're trying to separate a player from his very last chips. You worry first about winning the hand and then about winning the war, and here the move was to unnerve Hoang to where he started playing poorly, to where the thought that he'd laid down a straight would get in the way of everything else.

I wanted desperately to be the one to finish him off, but Dan Harrington beat me to it. He was at the table when Hoang folded, so he was probably moving in for the same kill. Remember, Harrington was a former World Series champion, so he knew how to pick his spots. Same kind of player as Hoang, too. Careful, tight, conservative. But cutthroat and ruthless when the situation called for it, with a killer instinct that didn't exactly fit with his quiet demeanor. Harrington caught a full house and put Hoang out of the tournament—in twenty-eighth place, with a $35,000 prize—and there was one less stack for the rest of us to worry about. One less player who knew what he was doing to stand in the way of the rest of us who knew what we still had to do.

Phil Hellmuth quickly followed, along with Men "The Master" Nguyen and all kinds of big-time players, as the consolation-prize money reached to $45,000.

I gave back some of my stack in the half hour or so leading up to the dinner break, but I held fast to my momentum—looking all the way past the $45,000 to the Final Table prize pool. We'd halved the field since the start of play that afternoon, and I was still in the thick of things, still sitting behind a big stack of chips, still liking my chances. There was a time when I would have been elated with a $45,000 payout, but that time was long gone. With perspective I might have been elated, but now, this deep into it, on an adrenaline high unlike any I'd ever known, I was gunning for that Final Table, where the prize money reached into six figures.

Here's how the chips were stacked after the fourth session of the day:

CHIP LEADERS: DINNER BREAK, DAY FOUR—8:15 P.M. ♥♣♠♦

Player	Chip Count
1. Boyd, Dutch	899,000
2. Vahedi, Amir	630,000
3. Thorson, Olof	576,000
4. Fitoussi, Bruno	572,000
5. Nguyen, Scotty	541,000
6. MONEYMAKER, CHRIS	516,000
7. Harrington, Dan	479,000
8. Ivey, Phil	456,000
9. Farha, Sam	455,000
10. Benvenitsi, Tomer	455,000
11. Watkins, Bryan	424,000
12. Jones, Bill	380,000
13. Nguyen, Minh	336,000
14. Grey, David	279,000
15. Lester, Jason	232,000
16. Deeb, Kassam Ibrahim	224,000
17. Luske, Marcel	199,000
18. Pak, Young	193,000
19. Lederer, Howard	186,000
20. Grigorian, Chris	158,000
21. Rosenkrantz, Abraham	102,000
22. Singer, David	45,000

PLAYERS REMAINING: 22

A lot of the players and hangers-on were talking about Dutch
Boyd during the dinner break, and Bruce and Dave and my father
had been hearing all kinds of things about him in the gallery during
the run of play, so they filled me in. Apparently he was something
of a boy genius. Graduated high school at about the age of twelve,
breezed through college and got his law degree at eighteen. For
some unknown reason, he'd turned his attention to poker. Started
up one of the first online poker rooms and helped to develop the
software that became the standard for most gambling sites. And yet,
for all his experience and education and accomplishments, he was
still regarded as something of a kid among these top players. He
had a kind of brash, dark persona, and he seemed to want to play it
to advantage at the table—and the fact that he had the chip lead in
what was essentially his first major tournament made him a target
of a whole lot of speculation.

I suppose folks could have scratched their heads over my position on the leader board as well, especially with the way I kept surviving these head-to-head showdowns with some of the more
established players on the tour. If I had any persona at all, I guess I
was thought of as a reckless rookie, someone who wasn't afraid to
take chances, to go for it, the odds be damned. And, I think, my reputation had shifted over the course of the tournament to where players who would have once welcomed the idea of sitting at the same
table with a rookie were now wary of facing down such a loose can-
non, on such a sustained momentum run, behind such a significant
stack of chips. I was unpredictable—just about the worst thing an
experienced poker player wants to see across the table.

Olof Thorson was the other wild card in this bunch. A big, gregarious man from Sweden, making some major noise in his first
tournament, he had won his own Poker Stars satellite to earn his
way into the World Series. I don't think there were too many players all that anxious to come up against Olof either, because he was
such an unknown and because he too had built such an impressive
stack. The two of us were the last surviving Internet players, and

I'm betting the Poker Stars people were really excited to have two of their own last all the way to this dinner break. It validated what they were trying to do online, offering serious poker to serious players all over the world, and it was a marketing bonanza. With just three tables going, and soon enough only two, the Poker Stars logo on the hats and shirts they were having us wear would be all over the ESPN footage.

I ran headlong into Dutch Boyd on a killer hand about an hour after the dinner break. He'd been whittled down to 650,000 in chips after making a couple hasty moves at pots he had no business playing, and I had managed to push my stack to 575,000, and we were about to collide in a big way. My strategy had been to stay out of the way of the large stacks at my table, but, strategy aside, it's always tough to look away from a hand you think you can win.

I was on the button and drew a pair of threes.

Boyd made a 40,000 raise, which I called. Both blinds folded. Soon as I called, Boyd flashed me a look that I took to mean he was pissed at me for stepping on his hand. I also took it as a sign of weakness. A guy with any kind of hand, he's not staring you down like you're stealing from him when you call his bet, so I put him on a bluff. Right then and there. My thinking was he had high cards but no real hand. Ace-ten. King-queen. Ace-jack. One of those hands that looked pretty good preflop, especially from a strong position, which may or may not get around to beating pocket threes. The rest of my thinking was that if the flop came under ten—that is, if all three cards were below ten—I'd move all in. Face cards, even a single face card, and I would throw my hand away. A ten and I was gone.

Anyway, that was the plan.

The flop came nine-two-five.

Boyd cheers. My move.

The more I thought about my all-in strategy, the more I didn't like it. We'd just passed the dinner break, there were only 20 players remaining in a field that had once numbered 839, and I'd yet to move all in from a lesser chip position in the entire tournament. Oh, I'd been all in a bunch of times—I'd been pushed there, and I'd done some of the pushing—but it was always from a position of strength. Here, with the weaker stack, I'd risk being eliminated, behind what was essentially a weak hand. Pocket threes was a strong enough hand to play, but I didn't think it was strong enough to play all in, not after I had come this far, so I recalculated my plan and bet 100,000 instead. I thought that would do it. I thought Boyd would choke on that big a stack and lay down his hand—and leave my blinds alone next time around the table.

But he didn't choke. He didn't lay down. Instead what he did was stare at me, for the longest while. He kept staring and staring and staring. It was a long, nerve-racking moment—especially when you see it played back on television. In fact, on the ESPN footage, they show Boyd taking off his glasses and turning directly to face me and flash a piercing, menacing look, only the producers seem to have edited that in for dramatic effect. He did indeed take off his glasses and glare at me at one point that evening, but it wasn't over this hand. It was over some other hand of far less consequence. This hand was dramatic enough as it was, without the need to punch things up in the editing room, and I sat behind my glasses for a full minute, trying not to move a muscle until Boyd made *his* move.

When he finally did, I was stunned.

He moved all in.

I thought, Aw, shit, what do I do now? I'd already considered pushing all in myself and rejected it as being too risky, but now I'd committed about 150,000 to the pot and was still putting Boyd on a bluff. It was tough to call him with just pocket threes, but it was even tougher to lay down when I knew I had the better hand. I just knew it. Felt it in my bones.

I'm guessing Boyd felt the same thing, and both our bones couldn't have been right. When I moved my chips around to make my 100,000 bet, I accidentally knocked over a couple stacks, and I figured Boyd mistook this piece of clumsiness for nerves or uncertainty. He picked up that I was weak—which I was, only not to the extent that he had apparently figured. It's funny how we poker players search so desperately for clues, trying to read the slightest tells from our opponents, to where we sometimes misinterpret a small misstep such as this one for a show of weakness—but hey, maybe that's what it was. Maybe I was subconsciously putting out that I didn't like the hand I was holding, that I didn't want to part with any of my chips.

I thought, Okay, I just got outplayed. It was the flip side to how things had gone with Humberto Brenes, when I'd moved all in on him from a stronger position after sensing weakness. Here I'd given Boyd a chance to come back over the top and steal my money, instead of pushing all in myself and forcing him to lay down—or at least giving him every reason to lay down. I went from knowing I had the best hand to thinking I had the best hand to not being too terribly sure of anything to fumbling my chips in such a way that Boyd had somehow managed to pick up on pieces of my uncertainty.

I also thought, Well, if I call him and I'm wrong and he has a high pocket pair, I can still catch a three on the turn or the river. I have an out. Even if he flopped a set, I can still catch an ace and a four to make a straight. These were long shots, both, but at least they were outs.

Two, three minutes, I debated my move. I went back and forth. The easy move would have been to fold, and I still would have had a healthy chip position, but the better move, the bolder move, was to call. I may have been outplayed to this point in the hand, but I could change all that with just one call.

I took my glasses off.

I rubbed my eyes.

I stood and paced.

There was nothing to shield at this point. I was torn with indecision, and it didn't matter if Boyd knew it. He had played his hand, and now it fell to me to play mine.

I called.

It would be either my last move of the tournament or one of my best.

I showed my hand and called out, "Low cards, dealer"—letting Boyd know that I put him on some kind of high hand.

He showed his cards: king-queen, which didn't amount to much against my pocket threes.

Still, Boyd seemed to have a hard time getting his mind around the fact that I had matched him all in with just a lousy pair of threes. "I can't believe you made that call," he said, shaking his head.

To be honest, I couldn't believe it either, but I was the heavy favorite in the hand going into the turn, about to bring the tournament leader down to size and vault myself to the top of the leader board. Long as the dealer didn't turn over a king or a queen.

"Low cards, dealer," I said again, pacing frantically on my side of the table. Hell, for all I know, I might have borrowed a page or two from Humberto's repertoire and done myself a little dance, that's how excited I was at this call. Really, it was huge.

The turn was a four, giving me a straight draw and making it even less likely Boyd would catch one of his cards.

I paced some more and danced some more and called out for low cards some more.

The river was an ace, and I about lost it right there. I'd made a straight out of pocket threes and turned the call of my tournament into just about a death knell for Dutch Boyd, who was left with only 75,000 in chips.

Man, the poor guy was just destroyed. Crestfallen, I guess, is the right word for what he was feeling. He even came over to me after the hand and wanted to know what I'd seen that let me make such a gutsy call. "What's my tell?" he said.

"Wasn't any tell," I said. "Just a feeling."

He kept pressing. "You must have picked something up," he said.

"No," I said. "Uh-uh. Just a gut feeling you didn't have a hand."

"That's a great call, man," he said, being more gracious than I could have been under just those circumstances. "I knew you didn't have anything either."

This last wasn't a dig. It was just Boyd being honest. And he was right. I didn't have much of anything, but it was enough. Barely.

Jason Lester, another top player who had taken the seat next to me immediately before this hand with Boyd, leaned over and whispered to me that it was one of the best calls he had ever seen in twenty years of tournament poker. This from a high-rolling Wall Street options trader who'd cashed—that is, finished in the money— eleven times in previous World Series events. It was, I thought, a helluva compliment, especially considering that the man didn't *have* to say a damn thing.

Whatever it was, I was the new chip leader, with 1.2 million in chips—for the time being anyway. I caught myself thinking I'd never had a million of anything—not even pennies!—and here I was looking at a stack of over a million in chips. It was tough not to think of these chips in terms of dollars, which is how it usually works at the casinos, because of course they had no cash value in a knockout tournament. Much as I might have liked to, I couldn't cash out and walk away with $1.2 million. There were roughly 8.7 million in chips circulating at these few remaining tables, the same total that had been in play since the start of the tournament—10,000 for every registered player—and I would have to grab a whole lot more of them (and find a way to hold on to them) if I meant to last out the day and see some six-figure prize money.

A couple hands later, after Howard Lederer was chased from the tournament in nineteenth place with $45,000 in prize money, Olof Thorson took down Scotty Nguyen to surpass me on the board. Amazingly, the two of us were on top of everyone else, and I scanned the room for the Poker Stars contingent to see what they were making of this unlikely turn. Two of their Internet buy-in players, tournament amateurs, running one-two in the main event of the World Series of Poker, down to the final two tables. They must have been thrilled, but their one-two punch didn't last long. In one of the very next hands, Thorson got caught in a strange bit of bidding with Amir Vahedi, a top tournament player who had been to the final table of this tournament a couple times. Vahedi was known for the way he chomped on an unlit cigar in smoke-free poker rooms like Binion's, and he would soon be known for his joyful exuberance at putting out Thorson on a scare card on the river. Vahedi had just lost a big pot, and he was famous for his aggressive play after a bad beat. Vahedi was dealt queen-eight of diamonds. He had a diamond draw after the flop, and not much else. Thorson had been dealt ace-king but was showing nothing. Vahedi pushed all in—a 600,000-chip bet to Thorson, who surprisingly called. I couldn't understand Vahedi's bet, but I *really* couldn't understand Thorson's call. Still can't. It's one thing to push all in with ace-king in the hole and nothing else on the board, but it's quite another to call off that many chips when you don't have any kind of hand. It was a stunningly odd move on Olof's part, but Vahedi was still behind in the hand. He had more outs than Thorson, but Olof had him high-carded.

The turn card was a two of spades—no help to either player. Both men were standing at this point, which was the default position on all-in calls this late in the tournament.

The hand was still Thorson's, but Amir could take it with a queen or an eight or a diamond on the river.

The dealer turned over an eight, and Vahedi went plain crazy. It really was a thing to see. He jumped up into the air and let out a joyous yell that has by now been repeated a couple thousand times on ESPN's highlight reel. He screamed, "Balls, baby, balls!" And then he ran around the table, wildly celebrating a wild pot—the biggest of the tournament thus far, at 1.6 million in chips. Put him in the chip lead, too, and just about slammed Thorson out of the competition. The poor guy went out on the very next hand—in sixteenth place, with $55,000 in prize money—he was so unnerved by Vahedi's eight on the river. He went from the chip leader to out of the tournament in just two hands, but that's how it sometimes goes in these late rounds of action. The space from starting line to top of the leader board can take four grueling days; the hard fall from boom to bust can take just a couple minutes.

No-Limit Hold 'Em, we remaining players took turns reminding ourselves as we watched Thorson exit, can be wonderfully cruel—and I imagine we all mumbled our private prayers that it wouldn't be so hard on us.

With Thorson gone we were down to fifteen players, split among two tables. I was playing at a table with Dutch Boyd, Amir Vahedi, Jason Lester, Dan Harrington, Sam Farha, and Marcel Luske, another Swede. The other table featured Yung Pak, David Grey, Tomer Benvenitsi, David Singer, Phil Ivey, Minh Nguyen, Freddy Deeb, and Bruno Fitoussi. And the weird thing was, no one seemed to be playing at the other table. I looked up every now and then, and they all seemed like statues. There was no noise, no excitement, no action. We were taking forever to get down to nine players, and folks were playing tighter and more conservative than usual, but I couldn't hear a thing coming from that other table. At our table we were firing money into our pot left and right. Stealing blinds. Not a whole lot of raising, but we were playing our hands. Those other guys—who the hell knew what they were doing? Watching paint dry, maybe. Waiting on the seven of us to knock each other off so the eight of them could advance to the Final Table.

At last, at about two-thirty in the morning, more than twelve hours in to this fourth day of play, Minh Nguyen got put out at the other table. That group had been playing six-handed, with Fitoussi and Deeb having already fallen, and our group had been playing five-handed, with Luske and Boyd biting the dust—and now, with ten players left, we all sat down at the same table. That hadn't happened too often during the run of the tournament, and whenever it had, it was only on a makeshift basis until a seat opened up at another table, but this was how the directors had the thing set up. There wouldn't be any seats opening up at any other tables. There was just this one table, nothing makeshift about it. It was like a semifinal table, without really being the Final Table. The deal was, we were supposed to keep playing until one more player went bust, after which we would break for the night.

Bust was a long time in coming. A little too long, if you go back and ask anyone who was in that room. It was late. Players were cautious. No one wanted to be the last player put out before the Final Table. Forget the significant bump in prize money. It was a point of pride. It was a great big deal to these tournament professionals, to make it to the Final Table. It had its own aura, its own prestige. Reputations were made on how many Final Tables you'd reached in your career. To come this close, to know that all you really had to do was sit back and not blow your chips until someone else beat you to it . . . I'm telling you, it made for some incredibly tense, tentative poker. Everybody was folding to raises, pretty much. Every once in a while, a short-stacked player would move all in, some impatient bigger stack would call, and the short stack would invariably win the hand. This happened a whole bunch of times, and you could literally see the shoulders of the other players sag each time they realized they'd have to keep playing.

The mood of the room was dog tired. The crowd had thinned from a couple hundred spectators to about fifteen or twenty. My dad and my buddies were still hanging in, but most everyone else had called it a day. A few folks were catnapping in their chairs. Really. Some of the players, too, seemed anxious to be done with things, making calls they wouldn't normally make, letting cards go that they would normally play. No one wanted to be chased from the tournament, but some of the remaining players were so spent that they wanted to be put out of their misery. It was going on four o'clock in the morning, and a few of these guys weren't used to playing sixteen hours straight, after a string of twelve-hour sessions. They'd had enough. Nerves were frazzled, and most of the players had pushed all in on good cheer a couple hours earlier. Everyone was flagging, and at one point a small group of players started working on the tournament organizers to amend the rules, upset tradition, and allow for a ten-handed Final Table the following day. It started out as good-natured small talk, but it quickly grew to where it seemed like a great idea all around. The thinking was, why not? Just send us all to our rooms and pick things back up the next afternoon. And I guess the Binion's contingent was dog tired, too, because it looked like they were actually considering it. Me, I left it to everyone else to hassle this one out. I could have played another sixteen hours. No reason to break from such storied tradition on my account. And yet, for a while in there, it actually looked like they were going down this road. I saw some tournament-director types pull out the Baggies they'd been giving us to store our chips until the next round of play. I saw people huddled in groups of two and three, like there was about to be a change in plans. I saw folks standing like they were done with sitting.

And then I saw my hand.

Ace-queen.

Like it or not, there was still some poker to be played, whatever these guys decided about the Final Table.

I raised—75,000. Nothing major at this point, just a stop-and-think-about-it kind of raise.

Phil Ivey called.

Jason Lester called.

I thought, Well, this could get interesting.

Understand, I wasn't planning on risking my tournament. No one ever plans on risking his tournament, but this is especially true at four-thirty or so in the morning when you're down to ten players and there are only nine seats at the Final Table. It's like a high-stakes game of musical chairs, and we all wanted a seat. I had a ton of chips—about 1.6 million. All I needed to do, really, was sit back and twiddle my thumbs until someone else made a move and a mistake. It would happen eventually. But at just that moment, my ace-queen was standing in the way of eventually. I wasn't planning on playing anything at all, but I had to make at least *some* play at an opening hand like that. Who knows, maybe if I brought a lesser stack into the pot—which I apparently had—I could knock someone out and we could move on.

The flop came queen-six-queen—a huge flop for me, to say the least. Giant. I didn't think anyone could touch me on the hand. Pocket sixes would have had me beat, but the odds against either of these two guys' holding pocket sixes were pretty damn long. I thought, Okay, this is my chance to put someone out. Jason Lester was short-stacked. Phil Ivey, arguably the most dangerous player on the circuit behind a big stack, had about 700,000 in chips. Lester wouldn't be a problem, because I had him in chips, but I wasn't really thrilled about going up against Ivey.

Like I said, first order of business was not to get knocked out of the tournament; second order of business was to take out another player and add his chips to my stack. The key would be coming up with just the right bet that I hoped would take care of both.

I bet another 75,000. Still not a particularly big bet, but I liked the symmetry of it. I liked the accessibility of it. I liked that it wouldn't take a bite out of me near as much as it could bite Lester or Ivey.

Ivey called.

Lester folded. I learned later, courtesy of ESPN, that he had a pair of tens.

I tried to put myself in Ivey's shoes as we awaited the turn. I was hoping he hadn't put me on that queen, even though I'm sure I was presenting that I had that queen. Why else would I have pressed the hand, at this late hour, from my comfortable chip position? I thought he had high cards, or a respectable pocket pair, else he wouldn't have stayed in the pot. Hell, he could have had that other queen and thought he was sitting pretty, never realizing that I had him with an ace kicker. Still, I thought the turn could be trouble. Either he'd catch his card and push all in or maybe he wouldn't catch his card and still make a play at the pot.

The turn card was a nine. No help to me. I had no idea what it might have meant to Ivey, but I felt I had to keep pushing the hand.

My gut response was to check, to let Ivey play into the pot and make his own mistake, but I didn't want to come off as weak. My three queens were still looking pretty damn good. But then I thought, Well, if he has a queen-king, or a queen-jack, which was about where I put him, I certainly didn't want to give him a free look at the next card.

Nines or sixes didn't even occur to me. Much as it pains me to admit it, I hadn't even gone there in my thinking.

As I was weighing my bet, I noticed Ivey fiddling with his chips. Now, with some players, this might have suggested he was itching to make a bet, but with Ivey you never know. He's cagey that way. I thought, Could mean something, could mean nothing. No, he didn't fiddle with his chips on the flop, but he was fiddling with them now on the turn. Did he catch his card? Was he waiting to pounce? Or was he just throwing out some mixed signals?

I bet 200,000, which I thought would force the issue. It would take Ivey down to about half his stack, but it wasn't enough to break him.

I never expected what happened next. He came back over the top on me and pushed all in. Apparently he'd been playing with his stack for a reason.

I thought, What the hell does he have? He couldn't have played queen-six, because I didn't think he would have called my opening raise before the flop with just a queen-six. Queen-nine, pretty much the same. And then I thought, for the first time, about those pocket sixes. That would have justified the first bet, and the second bet after the flop. Still, I kept coming back to queen-king, queen-jack. Could have even been another queen-ace, same as me. Those cards better justified his play to this point in the hand.

So I called.

Ivey flipped over his pocket nines, and I couldn't believe it. His full house beat the shit out my set of queens. I thought, How did I not see that coming? What the hell was I doing? Even if I didn't think nines or sixes were likely, I should have bet as if they were.

This stage of the tournament, you play those worst-case scenarios. Plain and simple. Now I was looking at going from one of the big guns at the table, right up there with Amir Vahedi for the chip lead, to worrying how I might last the rest of the night. I'd thought I was going to bed with over 2 million in chips, and now it appeared we might be playing for another couple hours.

I was devastated—and all kinds of showing it.

Ivey was elated, but he didn't show a thing.

He was a professional, and I was an amateur, and that's what we put out here when we showed our cards.

And then the river card came and changed everything: Ace.

The place just erupted. However much noise you'd think the fifteen or twenty remaining spectators were capable of making, and however much noise you'd expect to hear out of eight other thrashed and jaded poker players, that was about the size of it—and then some.

And you could plain forget about me. If I was over the top when I caught that third eight on the river heads up against Humberto Brenes, I was over the moon this time around. My full house, queens over aces, now beat Ivey's full house, nines over queens, and there was nothing to do but whoop it up and celebrate. It had to be about the wildest roller coaster of a hand any of us had seen in the longest time. Jason Lester had been ahead on the deal. I made my set and moved ahead on the flop. Ivey made his full house on the turn. And I came back with a stronger full house on the river.

It was the knockout blow of the tournament—and it came at the worst possible time for the most dangerous remaining player. Just before the Final Table. Just after Ivey had made a full house to apparently seal the hand.

You could play for a year straight and never see back-to-back, made-on-the-scare full houses quite like these.

Really, it was a tough, tough way to lose, and I felt for Phil Ivey. I truly did. But at the same time, I was giddy about it. Maybe I was a little punch-drunk from all those hours at the table, and maybe

I was a little more tired than I'd previously thought, but I was soaring. First thing I did, though, was cross over to Ivey, but he was too agitated to shake my hand. He just blew me off and walked to the other side of the room, and I thought, Hey, that's cool. That's understandable. The man had just lost an unbelievable hand that cost him his tournament, so he was in no mood for pleasantries.

Here again, people have talked about this as an example of my incredibly lucky streak, and I don't know how to respond. Was it a lucky hand? Hell, yeah, there was some luck involved, but both of us were drawing incredibly lucky, when you break it down. That was just the nature of the hand. Ivey had two outs after the flop, and I had seven, so who's to say who was luckier? We took turns getting lucky, is really a better way to look at it, and it just so happened that the cards ran out when the luck was on me. In fact, looking over the hand, I sometimes think Ivey's nine on the turn was probably the luckiest card of all for me—because without it I'd have bet my 200,000 and he would have probably laid down. Without that nine we might still be playing, the ten of us still jockeying for those nine seats at the Final Table.

One lesson I was happy to learn that night: It takes a long time to bag up 2.3 million in chips. That was the next order of business, for the nine remaining players to bag their chips and register the count with tournament organizers. I had time to catch a hug and some high fives from my dad and my buddies, but there was still some busywork to take care of before they'd let us go. Four-thirty, going on five o'clock in the morning, and they sat us down at a big-ass table and asked us to write out a short bio, which Binion's could use as part of their promotional material the next day. I figured they already had the information they needed on the other eight players, who were all tournament veterans, but they didn't have squat on me, so I took my time with the assignment. Wanted to reinforce my up-from-nowhere status and press the point that this was my first-ever "live" tournament. The Internet handle that had marked me as a fish on the first day would now be my strength, and it wouldn't hurt that I had the chip lead—at more than 2.3 million, nearly 1 million more than Amir Vahedi's second-highest stack.

It was about five-thirty in the morning when I finally spilled into the hallway outside the main room. I was dead to the world and on top of it at the same time. I shook some hands. I made a couple calls. Woke up Kelly back home. Caught a clap on the back from Chris Ferguson, a past champion and a fixture on the tour with his long hair and black cowboy hat, who took the time to congratulate me and tell me I was looking good.

Can't imagine that I really was looking all that good—certainly not in terms of appearances. I probably looked like shit, is more like it, but in the tournament he was dead on. I *was* looking good, and liking my chances, and desperate for a couple hours' sleep before we started up again at two o'clock the next day.

And as I took the elevator back upstairs to the twelfth floor, I allowed myself to finally think the unthinkable: *Play your cards right, Moneymaker, and you just might win the whole damn thing.*

CHIP LEADERS: CLOSE OF PLAY, DAY FOUR—FINAL TABLE ♥ ♣ ♠ ♦

Player	Chip Count	Seat Assignment
1. MONEYMAKER, CHRIS	2,344,000	8
2. Vahedi, Amir	1,407,000	1
3. Farha, Sam	999,000	3
4. Benvenitsi, Tomer	922,000	2
5. Singer, David	750,000	9
6. Lester, Jason	695,000	5
7. Harrington, Dan	574,000	6
8. Pak, Young	360,000	4
9. Grey, David	338,000	7

PLAYERS REMAINING: 9

8.
DAY FIVE

An honest deal makes its own friends.

—Benny Binion

The crystal guy was waiting for me as I made my way to the Final Table on Friday afternoon. I'd completely forgotten about my encounter with him before the start of play on the first day of the tournament, but there he was, standing outside the main poker room, looking out for me, making good on a promise that I guess had never fully registered. He was wearing another loud Hawaiian shirt—this one sea blue, with a funky tropical scene spread out across his big belly—and flashing a broad smile. He had a distinctive salt-and-pepper mustache, which made him look like a great big walrus with a receding hairline.

I made the connection right away, and I was glad to see him. Oh, yeah, right, I thought. The crystal. The guy had told me he'd give me one of his crystals if I made it to the Final Table. Cool.

"Remember me?" he said as I approached, extending his hand.

"Yes, sir, I do," I said, extending mine to shake it.

He handed over the same amazing crystal he'd shown me earlier in the week. "Didn't want you to think I'd forgotten about you," he said. "Congratulations, man. You've earned it."

I thanked him, best I could, even though I had about a million other things running through my mind. I really did appreciate it—both the initial gesture and the fact that he was now following through on it—but I couldn't really get my mind around it just then. I worked the crystal in my fingers and found myself drawn to the smoothness, the weight, the natural way it seemed to fit itself to my hand. We talked some, and as we did, I caught myself listening to what this man was saying. Buying in to this whole spiritual speech about the power of the crystal, the strength and confidence and positive energy it would bring. He was really into this stuff, and after just a couple minutes, he had me believing that this little crystal might hold the key to the rest of my tournament. He told me to keep the thing close, to put it on my chips or on my cards. To keep it within reach. Most important, to believe in it. I told him that I would do just that, and in this brief exchange, those million other thoughts fell away, and I found myself focusing on this crystal. In this one sense, at least, I suppose the damn thing really worked, because where I was once anxious and on edge, I was now calm and focused. Ready to go inside and play some poker. Have some fun. See what happened.

What happened, soon as the cards were in the air, was not much of anything. A whole lot of tentative play, same as the night before, and I suspected that things would go on this way until there was just one stack left. You don't make it to the Final Table at the World Series of Poker by being too trigger-happy. Recklessness doesn't cut it. Patience is the way to play it, and there was enough patience around that table to watch a couple coats of paint dry. Took me a few hours to find my game, and when I finally did, I was all over it. Put out David Grey, seated to my right in the seven seat, with one of my patented hands, a four-five, unsuited. Grey was on the button and raised with an ace–eight of spades.

I called.

So did Amir Vahedi, in seat one, with a five-nine, unsuited.

The flop hit my five, and the turn was a four, giving me two pair. Grey played it superaggressive, with just the ace to show for it, and he finally caught his ace on the river, but his one pair didn't hold up to my two, and he had to call it a tournament.

David Singer, in the nine seat, had already fallen on an all-in push to Amir Vahedi, so we were left with only seven players, and I was liking my chances a little bit more with each knockout punch. Didn't matter who threw it, long as someone else was taken out and I was left standing and no one else was made too terribly healthy in chips in the exchange. As we crawled toward the dinner break, I was feeling more and more confident. I was stealing blinds and growing my stack to over 3 million in chips. Trouble was, Sam Farha was building a similar head of steam. He pushed his way through our first four-way pot of the day—a hand that took more than ten minutes to play itself out, a god-awfully long time for a single hand that late in the tournament, and I set it out here for how it shows Sam Farha oozing the kind of quiet self-assurance I wished I had to ooze, although I realized that to the rest of the table it must have looked as though I was on top of things as well. Truth was, if I wasn't in on a hand, Sam was in on a hand. We were both playing from strength. We were the two big stacks at the table, and no one wanted to mess with either one of us unless he had a real hand. Hell, I didn't want to mess with Farha either, but soon enough I thought I had a good read on him and figured if I caught any kind of hand, I'd try to push him off his chips, take down his power some.

I was on the button, with a nine-ten, unsuited. Not much of a hand, but I thought I could do some damage with it heads up, and once the betting came around to me, it seemed no one other than Farha had been dealt anything stronger. He'd made a small bet— 80,000. Harrington called.

I called.

Amir Vahedi called, on the small blind. I hadn't counted on that.

The flop came four-six-nine, giving me the top pair on the board. It was a good flop, considering, and I was going to make a play at it.

Vahedi checked, which told me he wasn't on much of anything, probably a straight draw, given the flop.

Farha bet another 80,000, which troubled me. It wasn't the bet itself that set off alarms, it was how he made it. He was calm, almost too calm. I'd been watching his action for hours by this point, and I'd never seen him so still and composed. He was a cool, unflappable character, don't misunderstand, and he clearly wanted to present himself in just this way, but here he just seemed a bit cooler and a bit more unflappable than he had been all day long. I didn't know if this was a good thing or a bad thing, but it was most definitely a thing. Some new thing to consider. I wasn't too worried about Amir, because the flop had been a rainbow, and I thought that if he had caught any piece of it, he would have come out firing.

Harrington folded.

And because I wasn't liking Sam's action, I called rather than raised.

Vahedi called.

As it played out, I had the hand figured all wrong. Or at least I had Amir Vahedi figured all wrong. The turn paired the board with another six, and Amir immediately fired into the pot with a huge 300,000 chip bet. I don't think he even waited for that six to hit the felt before he pushed over those chips, so all of a sudden, I was putting him on a monster hand.

Farha called.

At this point I was putting Farha on a high pocket pair (aces, probably), and I was guessing I would have been beaten by Amir, and even so I would have gone up against either one of them head-to-head, but the thought of taking them both on with just my nine in the hole wasn't all that appealing, so I folded.

"You two guys have fun," I said.

The river came a blank, and Vahedi checked.

Farha bet 300,000, and Vahedi laid it down.

In the end Sam did indeed have a killer hand—pocket nines.

He'd made his full house and might have chopped my stack good if Amir hadn't been in the hand.

There was no saving me a couple rounds later. I was dealt six-eight of clubs, on the small blind. Farha raised, and I was the only caller. An ace came on the flop, and I checked. Farha checked, too, and I should have seen it for a red flag, because Sam always seemed to check when he flopped an ace. The turn gave me an open-ended straight draw, and I was putting Sam on that ace, so I checked, thinking he would bet into me. And that's just what happened. He bet, and I quickly called, thinking I was beat to this point in the hand, but that if I caught my straight on the river, he would pay me off big time.

Well, that was my first mistake. The second was what I did to make matters worse. The river came another ace and also made a flush on the board, so what did I do? I bet 400,000 into Sam, presenting that I had made my flush, when in reality I hadn't made my flush, or my straight, or any damn thing. Sam is not the sort of player you bluff frequently, or lightly, and here I was out on a serious limb. I was still putting him on that ace, and with two other aces now on the board, he would be sure to call. As soon as I made the bet, I wanted it back. I had to be an idiot to think I could bluff him off a hand like that, heads up—and, sure enough, I couldn't. He called and showed his ace, and I was screwed.

At this point, if I had to categorize my play, I'd say I was on the ropes. There was a stretch of time in there, running from about seven-thirty in the evening to about eight-thirty, when I didn't play much at all. I'd post my blinds when they came around to me, but I was hoping some of these guys would take each other out and I could wait on decent cards before making any kind of move. It wasn't like me to sit on my hands for any length of time, but I didn't see that I had any choice. I was surrounded by players who would have me for lunch if I tried to make any kind of move behind nothing hole cards.

When I looked up from this point of pause in my play, Young Pak had fallen from the tournament. He was put out by Jason Lester on an unlikely hand. Each player had an ace in the hole, and the flop turned over the other two aces. Lester took the pot with a king kicker to Young Pak's ten.

There were now six of us left, and Sam Farha had a considerable chip lead. As important, he was dominating play. It was his action, his tournament, his table, and I felt I needed to loosen things up if I had any hope of reclaiming the chip lead and the edge I'd enjoyed going into today. I needed to get back in on the action. I was frustrated. Goodness, we were all frustrated, with the way Sam was big-footing his way around the table.

Alongside this gnawing frustration, I was dealt pocket fours, and they had me thinking I could climb my way out of the hole Sam Farha had dug for me and put someone else back in there instead. I was on the small blind, and I raised into Amir Vahedi on the big blind. Vahedi swiftly pushed all in. Without even pausing to think about it.

I thought, Okay, pocket fours, not a terrible heads-up hand, especially with the cards I'd been drawing. And besides, I had to play *something*. I still had a sizable chip position, especially up against Amir Vahedi, who would be the next player to fall—only not on this hand. I nearly called Amir on this one. I came *this close* (I'm holding out my thumb and forefinger as I write this, to indicate an inch). I wasn't putting him on anything more than high cards, and my style all afternoon had been to play these kinds of small advantages, but I'd been getting burned by these kinds of small advantages time after time. I was on tilt, a little bit, from the way I was being beaten up by Sam Farha, and I felt I needed to give myself a breather—to shift gears to where I was once again in control, if not of the table, then at least of my own fortunes. So I laid down my hand, a hand I would have played nine times out of ten at any other point in the tournament, especially from the kind of chip lead I enjoyed over Amir Vahedi, and for some reason I took great comfort from this unaccustomed show of restraint. I fisted my new crystal in one hand as I pushed my cards across the table with my other and felt strength where there had been weakness, control where there had been carelessness, resolve where there had been all kinds of uncertainty. Really, in every other outward respect, this was a nothing lay-down. Pocket fours. No biggie. But in so many important ways, this was a turning-point kind of hand for me. This was where I took back my game. This was where I told myself that if I got beat, I got beat, but I would not beat myself.

This was about seven hours into our Final Table action, and most of us were fairly thrashed. The blinds had reached to 15,000/30,000, with a 5,000-chip ante, so with six players left, there was 75,000 in chips committed to each pot before any kind of action, and that's a whole lot of action and pressure to heap on top of an already pressure-filled situation. Remember, we'd been at this for a stretch of twelve-hour-plus days. All week long, with no letup, the stakes ratcheting higher with each passing hour. The night before, we'd been playing until four o'clock in the morning. And now here we were, looking at another marathon session. It was all about pace and stamina and convincing yourself you were on some kind of right track, so I seized on this lay-down like it was all-important.

And therefore it was.

Amir Vahedi would fall after another few hands, on a stone-cold 400,000-chip all-in bluff to Sam Farha that Sam either had the insight to read or the chips to play anyway. Vahedi had been dealt a four-six, and Farha an ace-five, and an ace-queen-nine flop all but sealed Vahedi's fate.

At this point in the tournament, we were allowed a short break whenever a player was knocked out, to accommodate the ESPN television crew. Someone comes around to interview the fallen player, and the rest of us are given a welcome few minutes to catch our breath and our bearings. I used the time to wander over to my dad or to Bruce or Dave and get myself a little reality check, see what the action looked like from their vantage point. A lot of players don't particularly appreciate these breaks, which can upset your rhythm and upend your momentum, but they worked pretty well for me. Gave me some time to put things in perspective.

Next significant hand came a short time later. Dan Harrington was on the button. I was on the small blind. Tomer Benvenitsi was on the big blind. (Amir Vahedi had been chased from the tournament on an all-in bluff to Sam Farha that didn't exactly work out the way he had planned.) Harrington made a small raise, which naturally set off all kinds of alarms in my head. Dan was the tightest player at the table, by a pretty wide margin, and most of us were in the habit of folding whenever he made a raise preflop. It generally meant he had a pocket pair or high cards or high suited connectors. It rarely meant he was bluffing.

I was down to about 2.4 million in chips, and I turned over an ace–two of spades, which for some reason I liked as an opening hand.

Wasn't much, but I called.

Tomer Benvenitsi pushed all in from his considerably smaller chip position.

Sam Farha, who had called the big blind, quickly folded.

Harrington folded. I learned later, from the ESPN footage, that he'd been playing pocket fours, which accounted for his small raise. Also wasn't much, but I guess he felt he had to start playing.

My first thought here was to follow Dan and Sam into the muck, but then I thought about it some more and wondered if I could pick anything up by twiddling my thumbs for a beat or two. I had played with Benvenitsi some on day four of the tournament, and by this point we'd been at it seven or eight hours at this Final Table. I thought I had a pretty good read on him which I might as well put to work here. So I checked him out, and as I did, I noticed that his arm muscles were in a kind of spasm. He's a big guy, Tomer Benvenitsi, and I could really see his muscles tighten up on him, and his shirt moving fitfully underneath, which told me he was nervous. I thought, Okay, is this an ace-ten kind of nervous or a two-seven kind of nervous? Lots of folks don't pay attention to how some players put out that they're nervous even when they're sitting with a killer hand, so I had to determine if Tomer's tells told me anything I could use. After a bit I saw him rock gently in his chair, back and forth, something I hadn't really seen him do to this point, and I took this as a sign that he was weak in the hand. I could have been wrong, but I didn't think so, and I started to look on this as my chance to take him out, to thin the herd by one other player, and I only had to risk another 20 percent of my stack to do so.

I called, and Benvenitsi flipped over a ten-jack, unsuited.

I don't think either one of us was liking the way that board was looking when we turned over our cards. We were each on nothing-special hands that we now had to play into something decent.

I caught my ace on an eight-ace-eight flop—a dead man's hand that I hoped would be my opponent's undoing instead of mine—and Tomer kind of sagged his great shoulders and seemed ready for the worst of it.

The turn was a nine, which gave Benvenitsi a nice straight draw and had me momentarily worried. I called out to the dealer, "Don't do it to me!"

The river was another nine, which kept my aces good and knocked Tomer off his straight and straight out of the tournament, and as I moved to shake his hand, I did a quick chip count in my head. I was once again over 3 million, for the second or third time that day, but still trailing Farha by a couple hundred thousand. I'd done my part in pushing some of these smaller stacks from our table, but I still hadn't managed to push Sammy off his lead, something I knew I would soon have to do if I hoped to have a chance in hell at the championship. The prize money kept growing with each knockout blow—Tomer Benvenitsi took home $320,000 in fifth place, and the next to fall would grab a fourth-place prize of $440,000—but I was well over worrying about the prize money. The money, at this point, almost didn't matter, because we'd shot past all the money in the world a long time ago. No matter where I finished, here on in, Kelly and I would be set for the next while. No, the only prize I had in mind was that first-place prize. I wanted that World Series bracelet. I wanted that exclamation point to this un-likely run. I wanted it all. And just then, at just that moment, this slick veteran who kept chomping on his unlit cigarette the way Ko-jak used to chomp on lollipops was very much in my way.

Also in my way were the two smaller stacks at the table, Jason Lester and Dan Harrington, and I took care of Lester soon enough. He had been like a gadfly in a lot of these Final Table hands—not much of a factor in any given hand, but always in the mix, always in on the action. He seemed like a nice enough guy and a smooth enough player, but we were at a point in the tournament where even the nice enough guys and smooth enough players had to fall if I hoped to keep playing. I didn't much care if I came across as nice or smooth, as long as I came out ahead. I bet 100,000 behind an opening hand of jack-queen, which Lester quickly raised 350,000. I called, thinking jack-queen was a strong enough hand to play heads up with such a commanding chip lead. I didn't even stop to put Lester on any kind of hand, just figured he was strong as well and we'd have at it.

The flop had my name on it: nine-eight-ten, which gave me a straight.

Lester pushed all in, and I immediately called.

We turned over our cards, and he knew he was in trouble. His ace-queen had me beat before the flop, and now the only cards that could beat me were king-jack, which would give him an ace-high straight off the flopped ten, but a third queen came on the turn, and he was done before the river.

With Lester gone, it was now down to Farha and Harrington and yours truly, and I reclaimed the chip lead a short while later in a showdown with Farha. I bet 125,000 to open the hand. Farha reraised to 350,000 from the small blind. Now, I don't care what stage you're at in a tournament, 350,000 is a whole lot of chips, but I was tired of the way Farha was pushing me around, and I had drawn an ace-four and thought to play it aggressively. The odds of Sam's sitting on pocket aces were all kinds of unlikely, and I just figured (stupidly, perhaps) that there were all kinds of chances for me to make my hand, no matter what he was playing.

I learned later that Sam had pocket queens, which had me beat before the flop.

After the flop was a whole other story: jack-three-ace, giving me high pair on the board and giving Sam Farha a whole lot to think about.

He checked, and now it was me with a whole lot to think about. So I thought. Hmmm. He'd just opened with what was probably the biggest opening bet I'd seen all tournament, and now he was checking. It was a sign of either weakness or uncertainty, or it was some kind of tactic that was beyond my thinking. I took it to mean that he didn't have an ace or a pair of jacks and that I was now ahead in the hand, so I bet 200,000. Enough, I thought, to give *him* something to chew on.

Now it was Farha's turn to think things over, and he did. Over and over and over. Sucked on that cigarette like it would give vodka—or at least some kind of clue what I was holding.

Ultimately he laid down his cards and I thought, Okay, Money-maker, you might have played that a little too wildly out of the gate, but you calmed down and let the cards pay you off. And it was a pretty big payoff—left me with nearly 4.3 million in chips to Sam Farha's roughly 3.6 million and Dan Harrington's half million or so, the kind of steep chip swing that could set me off on a momentum run in a shorthanded game.

Anyway, that was the plan.

Harrington doubled up just a few hands later—on my chips, which didn't make me too happy. I made an opening raise of 100,000 with an ace-queen in the hole. Dan pushed all in with a king-ten, and I pushed right back. I was playing superaggressive in this round, wanting to build on my lead and my momentum, but Dan caught a ten on the flop and took the hand. Lucky for me, he gave back some of those chips after another couple hands, when I flopped trip queens to his pair of aces to win another seven-figure pot and once again climb back over 4 million in chips.

Things went on like this for the next several hands. Harrington was up against it but never to be counted out. He always seemed to find a way to win a pot when he needed it most, and the longer we played, the more he needed it. Eventually, though, his chips ran out on him. He found himself with a strong diamond draw and a pair of sixes after a flop and moved all in against my pair of tens, which really was the only move he could have made at that late stage in the tournament. He was so far behind in chips that he had to play desperate and hopeful, which was a far cry from his usual style of cool and cautious. He was never one to risk his entire tournament unless he had the cards to back it up. He did just that a couple hours earlier, heads up against me, in a pot we wound up splitting. I'd been dealt an ace-jack and came over the top after a jack-jack-ten flop with a 100,000-chip bet. Dan raised me 100,000, so I figured I'd reraise him 200,000, after which Dan threw up his hands and reraised me yet again, pushing all in. I had a much stronger chip position, and I was liking my three jacks a whole lot at this point in the hand, so I called, and when Dan turned over his own ace-jack, we both breathed a big sigh.

Getting back to his latest all-in bet, behind that strong diamond draw and pair of sixes, Dan of course had no idea I'd made my own pair on the flop and had to like his chances enough to make some kind of move. It was now almost one-thirty in the morning on this fifth and final day of play, and, to bend and borrow an old gambling expression, all bets were off. Clearly he wouldn't have played this hand the same way on day three or day four, but it was just a three-handed tournament now, and he had to strike at anything that even resembled an opportunity, especially with the way he was down in chips.

In the end Dan didn't make his flush and was chased from the tournament in third place, with $650,000 in prize money—leaving me and Sam Farha to duke it out for the championship and leaving me assured of at least $1.3 million in second-place prize money. For the first time since counting out those five-figure payouts from the day before, I allowed myself to get caught up in the consolation-prize money. One million dollars! One million and three hundred thousand dollars, to be exact! How the hell do you *not* get caught up in that kind of money?

Just to reinforce the point, the Binion's folks put the tournament on pause for a couple minutes and wheeled out this huge cardboard box containing stacks and stacks of money and started to lay it all out on the table right in front of us. Made a big damn pyramid of hundred-dollar bills, reaching up to $2.5 million. I'd never seen that much money all in one place. Not even in pictures. And I sat there for a long beat, while tournament organizers arranged everything just so and tournament photographers started snapping away at the grand prize, and indulged myself in what was about to happen. Breathed in the moment to where I could actually smell that cold, hard cash. It gives off a smell, all that money, piled high at the center of a roomful of attention. Flashbulbs going off. People pointing at it, talking about it, inching close to get a good look at it.

Let me tell you, it was a monstrously huge distraction, but I wouldn't let myself be distracted. It wasn't like those short ESPN breaks for interviews with the exiting players. This ran somewhat longer, and me and Farha couldn't really move around at all. We needed to pose for pictures and talk to reporters and go through whatever motions the tournament organizers asked us to go through. In all, we were put on pause for a good chunk of time, and I hated to have to lose whatever momentum I might have had going into the previous hand, but this was the drill. I posed for whatever pictures they asked me to pose for, shook whatever hands were offered to me for shaking, and tried to stay focused. On winning. Second place might have promised $1.3 million, but at just that moment, it didn't mean anything. First place was everything. Second place was nothing.

We sat back down to play. I'd run my chip count to just under 5.5 million. Sam Farha was well behind, at 2.9 million, but he meant to do something about that straightaway, and in one of our first heads-up hands, he pushed me off a hand I should not have even been playing with what I later learned was a king-high spade draw that had flamed out with a king of hearts on the river. I bet strong after the turn, with nothing, but only checked after the river, still with nothing, and Sam came back with a 300,000 bet that forced me to throw in the hand. He outplayed me, was what he did, all the way down to 4.6 million in chips to his 3.8 million.

We'd play a total of twenty-eight heads-up hands before determining a winner, and it was impossible for either one of us to establish any kind of edge over that stretch. Momentum swung back and forth like it was on a pendulum. Whenever I made a push, it was usually the cards or my chips doing the pushing. Whenever Sam pushed, it was the cards or his considerable edge in experience. This was a guy who'd been down this road before. This was a guy who knew what he was doing, a veteran tournament player with tons of experience in high-stakes, high-end competition. Me? I was still playing in my first-ever tournament. I might have been five days and sixty marathon hours into it, and I might have outlasted the rest of the field, but it was still my first-ever tournament, and I couldn't help but think Sam had the advantage. Even when it was down to just the two of us and I was up nearly two to one in chips, I still put him in the lead. In my head Sam Farha was the odds-on favorite.

At about three in the morning, thirteen hours into this final day of play and about an hour and a half into our heads-up showdown, I turned over a seven of hearts–king of spades and made a 100,000 raise. A small raise, considering our chip stacks and the steep blinds, but it was a place to start.

Farha called.

The flop was nine of spades–two of diamonds–six of spades.

Sam checked.

I checked.

The turn was an eight of spades, giving me both a spade draw and a straight draw. I had no idea what it gave Sam, but I had to think, from his earlier betting, that it didn't give him much of anything either.

Sam thought different. He bet 300,000, which left me to lift my cap and scratch my head. As much as I thought about it, I couldn't put him on a hand, but I was liking the way the board put me on those two draws, so I raised 500,000.

He called.

The river was a three of hearts, which didn't take me to either draw. Hell, it didn't take me anywhere. The only thing I had to bet on was that Sam didn't know this. For all he knew, I could have made my straight with that eight on the turn. Could have made my flush there, too.

Sam checked.

So I pushed all in. I was up about 1 million in chips, so it's not like it would have busted me to lose the hand. It would have wounded me, that's for damn sure, but I'd still be in it, and I wanted Sam to know that I was willing to risk a serious wounding on what I was holding. Like I said before, Sam Farha is not someone you want to bluff lightly, or all that often, but I didn't think I could beat him without mixing things up a little. If I relied on the cards, just, I could be here all night. Or I could be out on the next hand. This hand hadn't offered me much but the chance to move in behind it, so I grabbed at it, hoping Sam would lay down.

Turned out, Sam sat and fidgeted for a while before making his move in response. He chewed on his cigarette. He fiddled with his chips. He started talking, which I'd noticed he sometimes did when he was rattled. It was that thinking-out-loud kind of talking. He told me how I must not have made my flush. He told me he didn't think I had a hand. He stared me down, hoping I would crack or twitch or grimace or show something, but I didn't move a muscle. One of the ESPN announcers said later that I was like a statue, just sitting there behind my shades, my ball cap pulled low, waiting on Farha to make his move.

Finally he folded. And he seemed to hate that he folded. Started talking, and in the chatter let it be known that he had folded a big hand. Why he wanted me to know this, I'm still not sure, especially after having seen the ESPN footage that showed him with a queen of spades–nine of hearts. The same flush draw I was looking at, but with the high pair on the board. I guess he got that I had been bluffing and wanted to take the opportunity to bluff me right back. Told me he had laid down a very high pair, which wasn't exactly how most players would describe a pair of nines, and when I pressed him on it, he said he had a pair of queens.

"Queens?" I said back. "There wasn't a queen on the board."

Farha simply nodded, with enough bluster to suggest a weather advisory.

"You had queens in your hand?" I said, making sure.

He nodded again. "I had queens in my hand," he said, which of course didn't match up at all with the way he'd bet the hand, but there it was. I just let it slide, figured I'd let the man tell me whatever the hell he wanted to tell me, let him vent and rail and steam in whatever ways he wanted, and it wasn't until some months later, when I had a chance to see the hand again on television, that it occurred to me he might have been talking about that earlier hand, when Dan Harrington was still in the mix, when I had bluffed Sam off pocket queens.

Even as I write this, I'm not sure what he was up to with this line of banter. Best I can figure is, he was tired, and maybe a little flustered. Next best is that he wanted me to know he had the cards to beat me and that sooner or later my bluffs would run out and his experience would prevail. It's almost like he wanted me to think he had *let* me win this one hand, to get me thinking it had been some kind of gift and that he had the power to bestow and revoke such gifts. Or some such nonsense. In the end, though, it didn't matter what he was trying to tell me, because I could just tune him out and play my game and let the cards decide who deserved to win.

Which is just what happened—on the very next hand! It was now going on three-fifteen in the morning, and I'd built my stake up to about 5.7 million in chips. Sam was treading water at about 2.7 million. I was dealt a four of spades–five of diamonds. I didn't know it at the time, of course, but Sam was dealt a jack of hearts–ten of diamonds.

Farha raised 100,000, which I immediately called. I'd had some good luck with that four-five, unsuited, as an opening hand, and I saw no reason to think it would run out just yet. Hell, it was the same hand I'd drawn earlier in the day, to chase David Grey and start me on my knockout Final Table run, and I reached for my special crystal and thought maybe it was some kind of omen. I mean, a four-five, unsuited, to take down my first opponent of the day, and another four-five, unsuited, to possibly take down my last . . . what were the odds?

The flop: jack of spades–five of spades–four of clubs.

I checked. It was a giant flop for me, no question, but I didn't want to appear too enthusiastic at this late hour. I wanted to see how the flop looked to Sam, to see if maybe he would bet into me.

Happily, he did. He must have thought he had the high pair on the board, and he bet 175,000.

I raised 300,000.

Sam, who'd been bantering for hours about how it would all come down to one hand, how we would never know when things would shake out or how the tournament would be decided, cupped his hands over his chips like he was preparing to push all in. It struck me then, and still, as a what-the-hell kind of bet, almost like he'd had enough already and wanted to force the issue, either way.

"Let's go," he said.

I thought about it for about a second. "I call," I said, pushing my chips toward the dealer.

"Let's go," Sam said again, as we turned over our cards.

He must have died a little when he saw my hole cards, but he didn't let on. He stood and took it like he had it coming. Me, I just stood. I took my hat off. Then I put it back on, backward, rally-cap style, thinking, No jacks, no jacks, no jacks. And, while I was at it, No tens, no tens, no tens.

The turn was an eight of diamonds—which meant that now a jack, a ten, or an eight could sink me on the river.

I was pacing by this point, and it seemed like it was taking just short of forever for the dealer to pull that final card.

The room was buzzing with anticipation. It was late, but there were still a couple hundred folks in the gallery. My father was still there, of course, and so were my buddies, and they were whooping it up and cheering me on as I was pacing back and forth, calling out, "No jack! No eight! No ten!" As if any of this would do me any good. Everyone, it seemed, was standing. All of them craning their necks to get a good look at the table. Wondering what the next card would bring.

Farha, for his part, was standing mostly still. It's like he was resigned to it. The bluster from just a few hands before was now gone. Even the bravado behind which he'd made this all-in call, with only jacks to show for it, was a memory.

He just stood and waited.

Everyone in the room was standing and waiting, but Farha was pretty much like a statue, waiting on the inevitable.

The river was a five of hearts, and it wasn't until a few beats later that I realized I had made a full house. All I noticed—and, more to the point, all that mattered—was that Sam Farha hadn't picked up a set or another pair, and I threw my fists into the air and let out a "Yeah!" that could have broken glass, and in the wild commotion that followed, I somehow found my father, and he collected me in a great big bear hug, and together we jumped up and down for a good long while, losing ourselves in what had to be one of the most sweetly surreal moments either one of us will ever experience.

"Yeah!" I shouted again.

"You did it!" my father hollered, from inside our hug. "You did it! You did it!"

He kept repeating himself, and it was a good thing, too, because, to tell you the God's-honest truth, I wasn't sure of anything at just that moment. Only thing I knew for certain was what my father was telling me, and if he was telling me that I had done it, then I knew it must be so.

CHIP LEADERS: TOURNAMENT RESULTS ♥♣♠♦

Player	Prize Money
1. MONEYMAKER, CHRIS	$2,500,000
2. Farha, Sam	$1,300,000
3. Harrington, Dan	$650,000
4. Lester, Jason	$440,000
5. Benvenitsi, Tomer	$320,000
6. Vahedi, Amir	$250,000
7. Pak, Young	$200,000
8. Grey, David	$160,000
9. Singer, David	$120,000
10. Ivey, Phil	$82,700
11. Nguyen, Minh	$80,000
12. Boyd, Dutch	$80,000
13. Deeb, Kassam Ibrahim	$65,000
14. Luske, Marcel	$65,000
15. Fitoussi, Bruno	$65,000
16. Thorson, Olof	$55,000
17. Jones, Bill	$55,000
18. Nguyen, Scotty	$55,000
19. Lederer, Howard	$55,000
20. Watkins, Bryan	$45,000
21. Rosenkrantz, Abraham	$45,000
22. Grigorian, Chris	$45,000

23. Waterman, Dennis	$45,000
24. Rose, Mark	$45,000
25. Nguyen, Men "The Master"	$45,000
26. Kastle, Casey	$45,000
27. Hellmuth, Phil	$45,000
28. Hoang, Chuc	$35,000
29. Ramdin, Annjano	$35,000
30. Plastik, David	$35,000
31. Shulman, Jeff	$35,000
32. Miller, Jim	$35,000
33. Wheeler, Stuart	$35,000
34. Lennard, Ken	$35,000
35. Geers, Robert	$35,000
36. Thomas, Harry	$35,000
37. Anastasyadis, Konstantin	$25,000
38. James, Kenna	$25,000
39. Zeidman, Cory	$25,000
40. Duong, Tam	$25,000
41. Brenes, Humberto	$25,000
42. Song, Kevin	$25,000
43. Hardie, George	$25,000
44. Jenson, Ood Erland	$25,000
45. Darden, Paul	$25,000
46. Jules, Bui	$20,000
47. Duke, Annie	$20,000
48. Johnson, Timothy	$20,000
49. Greenstein, Barry	$20,000
50. Inashima, John	$20,000
51. Allen, Matthew	$20,000
52. Dumont, Daniel	$20,000
53. Doumitt, Charles	$20,000
54. Gardner, Julian	$20,000
55. Chiu, David	$15,000
56. Studley, Julien	$15,000

57. Liffey, Rory	$15,000
58. Kaplan, Jonathan	$15,000
59. Reichert, Tod	$15,000
60. Nadell, Brian	$15,000
61. Atkinson, Bruce	$15,000
62. Shoten, Charles	$15,000
63. Rechnitzer, George	$15,000

TOTAL PRIZE POOL: $7,802,700

9.

THE MORNING FRIGGIN' AFTER

DAN RYDELL: Would you care to join us in the sport of kings?

DANA WHITAKER: We're gonna race horses?

DAN RYDELL: We're gonna play poker.

DANA WHITAKER: That's not the sport of kings.

DAN RYDELL: What's poker the sport of?

DANA WHITAKER: People who play poker.

—*Sports Night*

I've always believed that the level of drunkenness a man can justify in moments of celebration is directly tied to the long odds against having a damn thing to celebrate in the first place. Therefore, before I cop to the monumental drunk I put on just after winning the championship event at the 2003 World Series of Poker, let me put my situation in perspective—and, while I'm at it, let me remind readers that poker players were never meant to stand as role models for socially acceptable behavior.

I grew up around cards and gambling and competitive sports. (And, because my grandparents owned a liquor store, I also grew up around alcohol—a quirk in the nature-versus-nurture debate I could never quite shake.) There was "action" in almost everything in our household, and in my crowd of friends, but it never amounted to much beyond bragging rights and loose change until I went to college. There, after a stunning early run of good luck betting on sporting events, through campus bookies and offshore accounts, I hit a doubly stunning run of bad luck, piling up five-figure gambling debts in no time flat. I was down and out and otherwise up against it in every which way—and a few ways more besides.

I quit sports betting for poker, mostly as a way to cap my losses, and after a couple years of small-stakes neighborhood games and tutorial play online, I actually got pretty good at it. Got to where I managed to win a few dollars every here and there, which didn't do a whole lot to ease my various other debts (student loans, credit cards, mortgage, car payments) but at least kept me at something close to par on the gambling front.

Meanwhile I'd married my (sort-of) high-school sweetheart, earned my master's in accounting, landed a job at a top accounting firm, lost that job in the wake of the September 11, 2001, terrorist attacks on the United States, built a house in the suburbs we couldn't really afford, and eventually found a position as a comptroller for a small restaurant chain at a much lower salary.

Oh, yeah, we also had a baby.

In desperation my wife Kelly and I pared back our lifestyle. Double quick. We traded our new cars for clunkers. We borrowed money from friends and family. We stayed in, more often than not. We considered filing for bankruptcy. Somehow, through pluck and determination, we managed to keep ahead of our bills. We followed the advice of a local expert on financial planning. We stuck as close as we could to an austerity budget. I took on additional work as a part-time consultant and personal accountant and was looking at taking on more. Over time we managed to pay down our debt—from a high of about $50,000 to a more manageable $10,000, not counting the mortgage on our new house. Things weren't exactly looking up, but at least we were able to look ahead.

One night, as a way to kill the time, I entered a $40 satellite tournament on an Internet poker site where I often played. First prize was the entry fee for a $600 satellite tournament that offered seats at the 2003 World Series of Poker to the top three finishers, plus expenses. That's how it works in these satellite tournaments. You win the small ones for seats at the bigger ones. I won the $40 tournament and didn't think of it as any kind of big deal. I looked to the $600 satellite as a challenge, a chance to play against stronger players, more than I did a shot at a grand prize. The World Series seats were worth $10,000, but they had no cash value—which of course meant they had no value to me. I was more interested in the $8,000 fourth-place prize, which, after taxes and whatnot, would have taken a big bite out of our monthly debt service.

Somehow I found myself in position to win the $600 tournament, even though I was tempted to tank my last couple hands and finish in fourth place—the only in-the-money position that was truly in the money. Instead I let my friends talk me into going for one of the first-prize seats, as a once-in-a-lifetime thrill. They were monitoring the action online, wanting to see how I was doing, checking in over the phone during the run of play, and all kinds of excited at my chances. One friend in particular offered to stake me $5,000 in exchange for 50 percent of my winnings at the World Series, where there was to be a prize pool of over $7.8 million spread among the top sixty-three finishers. It wasn't quite $8,000, but it was $5,000 more than I had going in, and I didn't think I stood a chance to last out the first day of play, so I accepted the offer and played my way to one of the top three spots in the satellite.

Then, a week or so later, that same friend had to renege on his generous offer. Things were tight. He couldn't come up with the money. I was devastated. I wouldn't have shot past that fourth-place prize without that $5,000 pledge. I told my father about it, and he offered to contribute $2,000 to help make up the difference—using the same math, for 20 percent of my action. Another friend offered the same deal, and two other buddies scraped together $500.

The idea was for me to use the $4,500 to pay off some debt, but I never quite got around to it. I used the money instead to stake myself to some "live" poker-room experience once I got out to Binion's Horseshoe Hotel and Casino in Las Vegas, the site of the World Series tournament. I also blew about $1,000 of it at the sports book in the casino, on a couple of Major League Baseball games that seemed a sure thing at the time. The money ran out just as the tournament was starting, and I was no better off than I had been before I'd signed on for that $40 satellite on my computer. The $8,000 windfall I'd been hoping for had become $5,000, which then became $4,500, which I'd then frittered away at the poker tables and on a few baseball games. The live experience was invaluable, but it was experience I couldn't afford.

Still, I had a tournament to play, so I played like I had nothing to lose—which in fact was the case. The opening field was 839 players, most of them tournament professionals. Many of the other players were like gods to me and my poker-playing friends. Johnny Chan. Phil Hellmuth. Scotty Nguyen. In certain circles their names alone had the aura of Barry Bonds, Michael Jordan, Tiger Woods. I'd never played in a live poker tournament in my life, never even dreamed that I could, and here I was about to go up against some of the living legends on the tour. My goal—realistic or not—was to last out the first day, and I managed to land on a conservative table and nurse my chips to a comfortable lead. As important, I managed not to embarrass myself. (That would happen later.)

On the second day, the goal became to make it to the third.

On the third day, I wanted to last long enough to reach one of the in-the-money positions.

On the fourth day, I was gunning first for thirty-sixth place, which paid $35,000, then for twenty-seventh, which paid $45,000, then for the top eighteen, which assured me of winning at least $55,000, and then for the Final Table, which guaranteed a payout of $120,000. At some point, with the Final Table in sight, I stopped thinking about the prize money and started thinking about the championship. I wanted to win. The money had reached to where it was more than I'd ever imagined, more than I would ever need, more than I had any right to expect.

With each new goal, I had to reinvent my game. I learned on the fly. I shook things up. I played reckless one moment, conservative the next. No one knew what to make of me—and, frankly, I had no idea what to make of myself. I didn't recognize myself out there, staring down these big-time players behind my Oakley shades, playing at poker cool.

I was all over the damn place, but at the end of every session, I was also—miraculously, unbelievably—up among the leaders.

Along the way I did some damage.

I put out Johnny Chan, my idol.

I put out Humberto Brenes, one of the top tournament players in the world.

I put out Phil Ivey, widely regarded as the most dangerous player on the tour.

At the Final Table, I put out every opponent but two.

And at the end of an incredible run, at two-thirty in the morning on the fifth grueling day of play, I was looking at a first-place prize of $2.5 million. Even after shaving off a 45 percent share for my "backers," it was a helluva lot of money.

More money than I had a right to even dream about.

And much, much more than enough to justify the rip-roarin', stupid, shit-faced, I-should-be-ashamed-of-myself-but-for-the-fact-that-it-was-a-kick-ass-good-time drunk that came next.

Abso-friggin'-lutely!

Here's what I remember, from the butt end of that long night. I remember posing for pictures with Sam Farha and some of the Binion's folks, and drinking a champagne toast, and speaking to reporters who hung on my every word like I actually had something to say.

I remember sitting behind a pile of hundred-dollar bills—$2.5 million, bundled in stacks of $50,000—and feeling like I was in some movie and thinking, Man, is this a shitload of money or what?

I remember breathing deep and realizing that all those bills gave off a distinct smell—a rich, intoxicating scent that was heady as hell and pretty damn fantastic.

I remember grabbing one of those cash bundles for an abbreviated night on the town, before realizing that $50,000 was probably a little too much walking-around money even for what I had in mind and settling instead for $15,000, which was also probably a little too much walking-around money but seemed closer to reasonable.

I remember signing all kinds of papers and documents that allowed me to bank the balance with the casino.

I remember my father sharing a limousine ride across town with Sam Farha, who ended up taking his $1.3 million in prize money with him—in cash, in those same $50,000 bundles, stuffed into a cardboard box that he placed on the backseat of the car next to my father.

I remember racing up to our room on the twelfth floor of the hotel with my great friend Bruce Peery and throwing together our few things and pinching a few bars of hotel soap for souvenirs and racing back down to our own limo, which would take us directly to the airport for a 6:30 A.M. flight back to Nashville after we were done with our carousing.

I remember an entourage of about fifteen—me, Bruce, Dave Gamble, Lou Diamond and his handicapping sidekick, and an odd assortment of dealers and poker groupies and other folks who had variously attached themselves to our group over the course of the tournament—heading out into the Vegas night, looking for trouble, or action, or adventure, or some wild combination of all three.

I remember peeling off hundred-dollar bills like I had a million of them, which was hardly the case—I only had 25,000 (yep, 25,000 hundred-dollar bills!), and most of those had been banked back at the casino.

I remember going to some seedy strip club that I couldn't find again if my questionable reputation depended on it and buying drinks for everybody and throwing around ridiculous tips and running up such an outrageous tab in such a short stretch of time that my $15,000 stake wasn't nearly enough to cover it.

I remember hearing that we were about $10,000 short, and that the place would accept only cash, and that after a whole mess of what I thought were persuasive appeals from my old and new friends, insisting that I was good for the money, that I was after all the reigning World Champion of Poker and fairly rolling in it, even though I wasn't quite rolling in it on these premises, the manager was still intent on detaining our party until our bill had been paid in full.

I remember a girl, Tori something, a Vegas fixture who had been hanging with Bruce and our group for the last few days of the tournament and who was along for the ride and seemed to knew every high roller in town, calling 1996 World Series champion Huck Seed on her cell phone at about five o'clock in the morning and convincing him to come down to the club with $10,000 in cash to cover our tab—which he promptly and generously did, in exchange for my $10,000 check in return and a good story to tell his poker buddies.

I remember spilling out of the limo at the airport to catch our flight back to Nashville, the rest of our group in tow to see us off, and moving from beers to mixed drinks to straight whiskey in such rapid succession that most of us could no longer see straight or process a single clear thought or carry on anything resembling a conversation.

I remember stumbling through the airport and passing out facedown on the worn carpet by the gate agent's station, not giving a plain shit until some weeks later what I must have looked like.

I remember somebody waking me up and all but carrying me onto the plane, although whether that somebody was Bruce or Dave or some kindly airline employee, none of us can quite recall.

And I remember passing out again, this time from a more comfortable, seated position, in which I remained until our plane touched down in Atlanta for a couple hours' layover.

Don't remember much between Vegas and Atlanta, but eventually I came to and shook myself alert and figured I'd have to get my shit together before we landed in Nashville, because Kelly and our buddy Dave Whitis and a whole bunch of folks at the restaurant where I worked were planning some kind of surprise. Kelly kept asking when our flight got in—when *exactly*—so we knew that something was up, and we meant to be relatively sober enough to greet it.

There was a limo waiting for us at the airport in Nashville, and it took us straight for the Bound'ry, where two hundred of my closest friends and relatives and casual acquaintances had gathered to welcome me home. We all felt like crap, with headaches the size of the great state of Tennessee, but this was a terrific antidote. Really, truly, it was kinda nice. There were local television crews and reporters and people I hadn't seen in years, but mostly there was everyone I cared about and everyone who cared about me, all in one place to mark a wonderfully unlikely occasion that everyone kept telling me would change my life.

I wasn't sure I bought the change-my-life part, but there was no denying wonderful and unlikely. My parents drove out from Knoxville, and so did my brother and sister, and the place was filled with colleagues and running buddies and all manner of family and friends.

There was also some guy I had just played a round of golf with a couple weeks earlier, someone who'd been taking money off of me on just about every damn hole, shooting the shit, calling me a knucklehead, having himself a good old time. Hell, we both had ourselves a blast. We weren't supertight friends, but you ride around in a golf cart with someone for four or five hours, have a couple beers, lose a bunch of money to him . . . it's about as close as most guys ever get to having a real relationship. Which was why I was kinda surprised when I saw him at the party. Not surprised that he would be there, because he definitely fit right in with my other knucklehead friends, but surprised at how he acted. Sidled up to me at some appropriate moment and said, "Excuse me, Mr. Moneymaker, but can I get a picture made with you?"

I looked at him and thought, Whoa, what's up with *that*? It'd have been one thing if he was razzing me in some way, but he was serious, and I couldn't think what to make of it.

"Dude," I said. "We just played a round of golf. We drank some beers. We're friends. What's with this Mr. Moneymaker shit?"

"Hey," he said, all taken aback and checking himself. "It's nothing. It's just, I wanted a picture made with the champion. Thought maybe I could get you to sign it."

To me it was nothing, but to him it was everything—and this right here was the essence of what it meant to win the World Series. This was how the stakes had changed. A friend of mine wanted a picture and an autograph, and he was looking at me in a whole different light, and for the first time since the tournament wrapped earlier that morning, I was sober enough to realize what it all might mean. Forget the money. Forget the thrill. Forget the wild ride of it all. This was a big deal.

A big, weird deal.

And it would only get bigger, and weirder, from here on in.

AFTERWORD

An update is in order.

Turned out I was right about the thrill, and the wild ride, and the big, all-over weirdness that found me immediately after winning the 2003 World Series of Poker. And it's not like the weirdness or any of that other stuff had to go looking for me, either, because I wasn't one of those uptight, reclusive types. I wasn't shy and retiring, or cool, calm, and collected, or any such thing. And I don't think I was all that modest, either. That wasn't my nature. Invite me to a party and I'd be the first one there, showing off my WSOP bracelet to anyone who wanted to see it, sucking back beers and swapping stories with anyone who wanted to hear how I took out Johnny Chan.

Yeah, my world did a 180 on me the moment I took that final hand from Sam Farha, no question, but it wasn't until ESPN started airing its edited coverage of the tournament in August 2003 that I was turned all the way around. Somehow, in the way the footage was produced and slick-packaged for cable television, I came across like the love child of Cinderella and Rocky Balboa, conceived on a poker table at the stroke of midnight and set loose on an American public that suddenly had a thing for Texas Hold 'Em. Like it or not (and I'm still not sure where I check in on this score), I came across as the poster boy for our mounting obsession with poker, and the what-the-hell, against-all-odds, hope-against-hope attitude I brought to the tables at Binion's seemed to reflect a national mood.

Anyway, that's what I was told. (What the hell did I know?)

Turned out, too, that I was a poker player, after all. Hadn't counted on that. Hell, I didn't even see it coming. Remember, the main event at the 2003 World Series was my first-ever live tournament. Best-case scenario, it was a chance to scramble my way out of some credit card debt if I could catch a good run of cards. Worst-case scenario: a good time that might yield a couple decent stories and some free Poker Stars gear. I'd played in a neighborhood game for a couple years, and I'd played a ton of hands online, but up until that week in Vegas I never really thought of myself as a poker player. I was an accountant/bookkeeper for a small chain of Nashville restaurants. I was a husband and father. I was a good ole hard-charging Tennessee alum, always up for a good time and a favorable betting line. Like I said, I played poker, but I wasn't a *player*, not by any stretch. I wasn't a player the way Chris Ferguson was a player. I wasn't a player the way Howard Lederer was a player, or Dan Harrington, or T. J. Cloutier. At least, I hadn't thought of myself that way until the World Series, and now that was pretty much all I could think about. Now, I wasn't fool enough to think of myself in the same breath as any of those poker legends, but I did start to think of myself as a player, and I did start to carry myself as a player, and I did start to sign autographs as if I was a player (apparently, the jokers and aces from a fresh deck are to poker players what an official major league baseball is to Barry Bonds), and I did start to play in a mess of tournaments—with mixed to positive results.

And then my world began to turn all over again. ESPN started airing the hell out of its World Series footage. Repeated it over and over, and each time out more and more people watched. Again and again. The producers had cut the five days of play into an eight-part series, and they just ran it into the ground. I think they showed it a couple dozen times before the end of the year, and a couple dozen times more by the following spring, and since I emerged as one of the stars of what was now being treated like a prime-time television drama, it got to where I couldn't walk through an airport or step into a hotel lobby without being recognized and pumped for questions and pressed for autographs and insights and anecdotes and otherwise glad-handed by everybody who had ever played a hand of poker.

And I wasn't complaining. No, sir. I gobbled up the fuss and attention, but after a while all of that fuss and attention changes things, at least a little bit. It got to where I couldn't sit down at a poker table without folks gunning for me because they thought I'd had a run of lucky hands and wasn't much of a player at all, or because they wanted to be able to tell their buddies back home that they'd knocked out the reigning World Series champion. I had an endless string of invitations to play in private neighborhood games, in high-stakes regional games, in sponsored tournaments at casinos across the country. If I wanted to, I could have sat down at a different table every night of the week, and one day toward the end of 2003 I looked up and realized that this was pretty much what I had decided to do. Like I said, I was a poker player, after all.

But Kelly hadn't married a poker player. And I hadn't passed myself off as one, either. That wasn't the lifestyle either one of us was expecting when we threw in together—and it certainly wasn't the lifestyle either one of us was seeking. Actually, as I've written earlier, I wasn't much of a catch before I set off on this poker whirlwind, but at least I was home. At least we were together. Poker changed that, I'm sad to say—in little bits, at first, but soon enough in big, serious ways that left us thinking we'd try things apart for the next while, see how that goes.

Without really realizing what was happening, I'd thrown in on the professional poker circuit in such a way that I couldn't keep things going at home, or at work, or anywhere else but at the tables. Everything about me was up for grabs—and it all had to do with poker, with constantly thinking the next big pot was only a couple hands away. So that's what I did. I played poker. I gobbled up all of that fuss and attention, and it bit right back. I was powerless against it, and at the same time empowered by it, if that makes any sense. (No, I don't suppose it does . . . how could it?) I busted out early in a couple of major tournaments, but then I started to turn things around. Took second place in the high-profile Shooting Stars tournament out at the Bay 101 Casino in San Jose, California, which carried a prize of $200,000—and after winning that $2.5 million grand prize at Binion's I guess I took it in stride. And it liked to kill me that I took it in stride. I mean, come on! Two hundred thousand dollars! The kind of money it would have taken me five years to earn as an accountant/bookkeeper, and here I was hauling it in like I had it coming.

I gave notice at work. Helped my buddies at the restaurant find and train my replacement. This on the theory that in order to do one thing well I needed to give it my full attention. I had been letting things slide at work, and I wasn't completely on top of my game the way I needed to be in order to play consistently well at these tournaments, so I weighed my options and sided with poker. Back of my head, I kept hearing that line from that "Woodstock" song—"caught in the devil's bargain"—and guessed that I must have made a side deal with the poker gods during my run at the World Series, one that left me no choice but to move *all in*.

So that's the short version of what happened to me in the wake of the 2003 World Series. That's the upshot. I blinked, and my life was transformed. I still loved my wife and baby daughter, but I was caught in this mad swirl and I felt like I needed to ride it out. It tears me up inside that that's how it worked out, but that's how it did. And so, torn, I threw in with Harrah's, the great hotel-casino chain that had purchased Binion's shortly after the 2003 tournament, and started making appearances at their couple dozen casinos across the country. I became a kind of ambassador for Poker Stars, appearing as a featured player on poker cruises and in regional tournaments. And I cut some endorsement deals that kept a nice chunk of money coming in, enough to cover me if I flamed out at every damn tournament—and enough to take care of Kelly and Ashley, even as I seemed content to crash on my friends' couches or in comped hotel rooms and to subsist on a diet of chips and beer and all-I-could-eat buffet food.

It took me a while to get my game going, so the guaranteed money was key. And, since this is a book about my poker experiences more than it is a book about my personal experiences, I'll try to keep the focus on the tables, where I came to realize I was a completely different player than I had been just a few months earlier, when nobody knew who I was and nobody bothered me. (Hell, nobody cared.) All of a sudden, everybody knew who I was and I found myself playing a more conservative game. I had to, just to survive, because reckless doesn't cut it when everyone else at the table is gunning for you. It was funny to me how some of the rookies and amateurs came gunning for me in a way they would have never gone gunning for Phil Hellmuth or Scotty Nguyen. Those guys, they'd stay out of their way, but they came after me—I guess because they saw me as another rookie or amateur, same as them. As a result, I found myself going head-to-head on almost every hand I wanted to play. I couldn't steal any blinds or bully someone else's raise the way I liked to do, because there was always someone willing to call my bet. Course, when I say *always* I suppose I'm exaggerating a bit, because I was able to push my way to a pot from time to time, but it did seem like folks wanted to tangle with me more often than not, and it did affect the way I approached each hand, and it did play with my head a little bit. But I don't mean to complain. It was just another adjustment I needed to make, so I set about making it.

The 2004 World Series of Poker loomed on my calendar like Christmas, and as the date approached I was anxious and antsy and pumped and good to go. It would be a great, validating thing, I thought, to post another strong showing at the World Series and send the message that I wasn't some sort of fluke or one-hit wonder.

Trouble was, I didn't exactly take good care of my chances going in—and I certainly didn't take good care of myself. I went out to Vegas with a couple of buddies about a month ahead of the main event, meaning to play in a bunch of satellite and preliminary events, and layering in enough all-night drinking and partying to take away any advantage I might have had as the reigning champion. The previous year, those satellite tournaments and side games had been all-important as I looked to get some "live" poker room experience, but this time around they were more of a hoot. And I did okay despite myself. I played in seven different preliminary events, and finished in the money in a No Limit Hold 'Em event, and in tenth place (one position shy of the final table) in a Pot Limit Omaha event. In all, it was a solid, respectable showing—and to my mind, it was doubly respectable for all the merrymaking I managed to squeeze in between hands.

Vegas was just busting with poker players. The 2004 World Series was like the Super Bowl, Mardi Gras, the Daytona 500, and the Fourth of July all rolled into one enormous party. The numbers tell the story. In 2003, there were 839 players registered in the main event, eclipsing the previous high-water mark by a couple hundred, and a total prize pool over $7.8 million. In 2004, there would be 2,576 players entered in the main event, with a total prize pool just over $24.2 million. That was an astronomical leap—almost too big to comprehend, and too much for the tournament organizers to accommodate. The main floor at Binion's was jammed, with tables occupying every available inch of floor space, and the downstairs area was overflowing as well. You couldn't move for trying against such a swelling sea of people—and if you add to the sheer mass the fact that a great many of these folks were just happy to be there and drink and whoop it up and rub shoulders with some of the legends of the game, you can begin to understand some of the chaos and confusion all around.

And I was fat in the middle of the whole damn deal. Not to blow smoke up my own butt, but everywhere I turned folks seemed to greet me like they'd known me my entire life. Some of the veterans joked that it was my fault the event had exploded in just this way, while some of the rookies and wannabes thanked me for giving them reason to hope they had a chance in hell. And everyone and his mother wanted to buy me a drink, to where if I'd have taken them all up on the offer I could have lubricated a giant toga party and still had enough booze left over to leave some of the hardest-chargers in the throes of alcohol poisoning. As it was, I took enough of them up on it to leave myself fairly fried, and reeling.

Man, it was an incredible, intoxicating scene—a blast and a half—and as the preliminary events began to wind down and Binion's began to swell in the final days leading up to the main event I tried to get my head around it. Against such an enormous, unpredictable field, there was no sure way to play it. Anything can happen. That had been the mantra of this World Series for years, but it was never more fitting. *Anything can happen.*

No shit.

Very first hand of the main event might have set the tone. There was no ante in this first round of play, and the blinds were at 25/50 to start. I'd been up until six that morning, celebrating my top-ten finish in the Pot Limit Omaha tournament, had caught just a couple hours of fitful sleep before this first round, and was holding back a hangover the Hoover Dam would have had a hard time controlling. I was seated at a table along the rail on the main floor, with eight other players I didn't recognize or know the first thing about. Internet players, mostly—like I had been just one year earlier—and I hated that I was so quick to dismiss them as Internet players, but there it was. I was the 2003 World Series champion, and I was tired and unfocused and probably still a little bit drunk from the night before, and if I wanted to write these other players off as fish, then that's what I would do.

I was dealt ace-two of diamonds. The player seated to my right made a 300-chip raise, which I quickly called. Another player seated to my left also called.

The flop was an ace of hearts and two middle diamonds, leaving me with the nut flush draw and high pair on the board and every reason to go after this first pot as if it might set me up for the next while.

Guy to my right bet 300.

I called. I put him on a pocket ace of his own, just to be on the safe side, and I still liked my chances.

Guy to my left called.

The turn card was another diamond, giving me my flush and the best possible hand to this point.

Guy to my right bet 1,000.

I called.

Guy to my left called.

Just like that, I was looking at a pot of over 5,000 chips, and I thought back to the first table on the first day of the 2003 tournament and realized I was in very different company this time around. The year before, we must have played a couple dozen hands, with bets and raises at no more than three times the big blind, before we'd put so many chips into the middle, total, and here we were right out of the gate, playing fast and loose and like there was no tomorrow. And I guessed that, for most of us, there would be no tomorrow—and even in my bleary-eyed stupor it never occurred to me to count myself among this group.

The river was a low club that didn't pair the board and left me with the nuts.

Guy to my right checked.

I bet 3,000—three times the biggest raise to this point, which I thought was just the right amount to press the issue.

Guy to my left folded.

Guy to my right called, firing another 3,000 chips my way, and before I could even catch my breath and my bearings I had over 16,000 chips and had taken a big bite out of two other stacks at my table.

I thought, This is going to be cake. And yet I seemed to want to have my cake and eat it too, and set off on a run of hands where I tried to bully the other players a little too much, where I tried to raise a little too much, where I tried to reraise a little too much, and after just a couple hours I'd given back whatever momentum I thought I'd won along with that first pot to where I was just another player at the opening table, trying to make it to the next round.

Three hours later, with the blinds up to 50/100, I caught an ace-king I thought might shake things up and turn things back around. You have to realize, I was really dragging at this point in the tournament, treading water at about 15,000 chips, slowly giving back the ground I'd gained on that opening hand. These hole cards were about the best I'd seen all day, so I figured I'd make some kind of move. Guy to my right must have been liking his hole cards, too, and figuring the same, because he pushed the bet to 400 before it came around to me.

I called.

Guy to my left called.

Wasn't much to think about just yet. You catch an ace-king, you call.

The flop was ace-seven-four, all different suits, giving me high pair on the board and a whole lot to like about the hand.

Guy to my right checked, and that whole lot to like was looking better still.

I bet 1,200, thinking I might press the point before the turn.

Guy to my left folded, which right away told me I might have pressed a bit too much, a bit too soon, but then the guy to my right came back over the top and pushed all in.

I thought, Whoa, where the hell did that come from? Really, it surprised the plain crap out of me. If anything, I'd been thinking my 1,200-chip bet might have been a little too aggressive, and this guy pushed in about 12,000 chips to set me straight.

So I gave it some thought. I had this guy by about 3,000 chips, so it's not like he could have put me out on this hand, but that didn't make my decision any easier. I was bone-tired, and still dragging from the night before, and yet I was determined to plow through this first day of play. If I could get a decent night's sleep, I felt sure, I'd be fresh for tomorrow, and back on my game.

I put this guy on pocket sevens, or possibly an ace-king, ace-queen, ace-jack of his own. I had to put him on something. I didn't think he had pocket aces, not least because they'd be the last two aces in the deck and the odds ran considerably against, but because he'd thrown down his first bet pretty damn quick. All day long, he had been tentative when he had the cards, thoughtful, and on this hand he was a little trigger-happy. Must be he'd flopped a set of sevens, is why he was moving all in. That, or he was liking his pair of aces a couple thousand chips more than I was liking mine.

After about three minutes, I called. That's a helluva long time to wait out a call, and when I was in its middle it felt like three months. I'm still not sure why I called, or what I was thinking, and if I had any kind of opening day strategy this move didn't seem to want any part of it, but there I was, pushing in a whole mess of chips and wondering what the hell I was doing.

Guy to my right turned over pocket nines, and I allowed myself a long sigh. I'd totally misread him, and I'd probably misplayed my hand, but for the moment it looked like I might skate on by and put this guy out of the tournament.

The turn was an ace, which nearly locked things up for me. The only card that could have beaten me at this point was a nine, which would have given this guy a full house, so I was sitting on my hands to keep from reaching for those chips in the center of the table.

Sure enough, the river was a nine, and the guy to my right hauled in a pot I had no business playing—and no business losing, considering my chances after the turn.

But there it was.

Man, it was tough to recover from such a bad beat, especially when I wasn't all that focused. Any other day, I might have found a way to scramble back, but I let it cripple me, to lose such a big pot in such a roller-coaster way, and I let the other players see that I'd been thrown. I was easy pickings, here on in, and I nursed my few remaining chips like they were all-important—although in truth, at just that moment, I can't say that they were. I'd gotten to that place in my thinking where the tournament itself was no big deal, where posting that good showing I'd dreamed about for the past twelve months now took a backseat to getting some sleep. And it's been my admittedly limited experience that when you're resigned to losing there's nothing left to do but lose.

Next big hand came about an hour later, on the 100/200 blind. I caught an ace-ten of spades, and I pushed the bet to 600.

Guy to my left (a *different* guy to my left) called.

The flop: king of diamonds, king of spades, nine of spades.

I went from looking at nothing more than a promising hand to a nut flush draw, which I realize now still wasn't much more than a promising hand. I played it anyway, pushing in another 600 chips.

Guy to my left didn't even think about it before pushing all in, and I hardly thought about it before pushing right back. I might have, though. Lord knows, I should have. I was the short stack, by a whole bunch, so if I was wrong on this hand I was done. But that right there was my problem. Whatever momentum I might have had after that opening hand about four hours earlier was now replaced by a momentum of a different kind. I was on a downward spiral, and resigned to it, and playing like I had nothing to lose. Truth is, I didn't have the first idea what this guy might be holding. My call was a classic what-the-hell? bet, with me thinking I'd already thrown 1,200 chips into this pot, and I had only 1,800 left, so I might as well look to double up or go home. Wasn't much of a play, but it was all I could manage.

Guy turned over king-jack, and I knew I was toast, and when the turn card came a nine I was burnt toast. There was no card on the river that could have beaten his full house, so I was dead, and done.

My first thought was, Thank God, now I can go to bed. That

was pretty much my second and third thought, too—that's how thrashed I was at just that moment. It's only been in the months since that I've wondered what might have been, how my tournament could have turned differently if I'd taken better care of myself going into that first round of play, if I'd cut back on some of that hard-charging and partying and paid attention to what I was doing. I thought back to the year before, when I'd gone in fresh and focused, and wished like hell I'd thought to take the same approach on this second pass, but the great thing about poker is that it offers up a never-ending series of beat-yourself-over-the-head life lessons, don't you think? What works one hand doesn't always work the next. Sometimes good enough is good enough, and sometimes it falls far short. Sometimes you play the odds and sometimes the odds play you. Don't take life or love or poker for granted, because there are bad beats all around. And on and on.

But the real lesson took a while to sink in, and here it is (I think): there's always next year.

Spoken like a true poker player, don't you think?

APPENDIX A:
CRIB SHEET 1

THE RELATIVE VALUES OF POKER HANDS

For the beginning poker player, and the self-styled veteran who's never quite committed these hands to memory, I include this standard ranking of poker hands, presented from strongest to weakest. Apprentice players, please note: Aces can be high *or* low, but not both, and high cards (or *kickers*) determine a deadlocked hand.

ROYAL STRAIGHT FLUSH
 Example: 10H, JH, QH, KH, AH

STRAIGHT FLUSH
 Example: 2D, 3D, 4D, 5D, 6D

FOUR OF A KIND
 Example: 9D, 9C, 9H, 9S, KH

FULL HOUSE
 Example: JD, JH, JS, 6C, 6D

FLUSH
 Example: 3S, 6S, 7S, JS, KS

STRAIGHT
 Example: 7C, 8D, 9D, 10H, JC

THREE OF A KIND
    Example: 3C, 3D, 3H, 7H, AS

TWO PAIR
    Example: AD, AC, 4H, 4C, 5S

ONE PAIR
    Example: 8C, 8S, 2C, 4H, JH

HIGH CARD (NO PAIR)
    Example: 6D, 7C, 10S, JC, AH

APPENDIX B: CRIB SHEET 2

A SHORT COURSE ON TEXAS HOLD 'EM

Texas Hold 'Em has quickly become the game of choice in tournament play. It's probably one of the simplest variations of poker out there, but at the same time, it can be a subtle, complex game that takes years to master at the world-class level. Hell, it can take years to master at the local, neighborhood-game level as well. Its fast action appeals to tournament organizers and players—and the knockout, no-limit version of the game is ideally suited to the tournament format.

Here's how it works: Texas Hold 'Em is a standard, seven-card poker game that allows players to build the strongest five-card poker hand from any combination of hole (or *pocket*) cards and community cards.

The deal moves clockwise around the table after each hand. In tournament play, with a house dealer, the position is determined by the dealer button—a small disk, about the size of a poker chip, that moves from player to player after each hand. As in most other poker games, the player seated in the dealer position (or, in Hold 'Em terms, *on the button*) will be the last to act in each round of betting—with the Hold 'Em exception of the first round of betting, which is explained below.

The player seated to the immediate left of the dealer is in the *small blind* position. The player seated to that person's left is in the *big blind* position. Prior to the deal, both blinds are required to post live bets on the coming hand. The bets are considered "live" because they initiate the first round of betting. They're considered "blinds" because they are posted before players have an opportunity to see their cards. (In some games Hold 'Em players also ante before each round of play, further increasing the action before active betting begins.)

Unlike a traditional ante into each new pot, the blinds are used to jump-start and stimulate betting on each hand, while at the same time allowing players seated in other positions to sit out the action until they are dealt more favorable hole cards. Typically the big blind will be double the amount of the small blind. In home games these amounts are established before the start of play. In tournament action the blinds are usually raised at predetermined intervals. In the World Series of Poker, for example, the blinds increase every two hours—beginning at $25/$50 and reaching as high as $50,000/$100,000 by the Final Table.

Two cards are dealt facedown to each player. The betting action resumes with the player seated to the left of the big blind and continues clockwise around the table. As in other poker games, players may fold, check, bet, or raise in turn. For this first round of betting, the big blind has the privilege of last action and can fold, check, call, or raise the previous bet.

Following this first round of betting, three community cards are dealt faceup. These three cards are known as the *flop,* and they begin another round of betting, starting with the player seated to the left of the dealer.

Following this second round of betting, a fourth community card is dealt, known as the *turn* card—or, in some circles, *fourth street.* Another round of betting takes place.

Following this third round of betting, a fifth and final community card is dealt, known as the *river* card—or, in some circles, *fifth street.* A final round of betting takes place, after which players remaining in the hand show their cards and the highest-ranking five-card poker hand takes the pot.

In No-Limit Hold 'Em, players can bet all of their remaining chips at any time following the big blind, as long as the action falls to them. These bets, known as *all-in* bets, allow players to risk their entire stake on a single hand, even if they do not have enough chips to cover a preceding bet. For example, a short-stacked player may push all in to call a bet he couldn't otherwise cover. By pushing all in, he is able to remain in the hand, while a side pot is established to account for the difference between the initial bet and the all-in call. Similarly, a large-stacked player may push all in against a shorter-stacked opponent, forcing that player either to risk all of his remaining chips to stay in the hand or to fold his hand.

APPENDIX C: CRIB SHEET 3

THE RELATIVE VALUES OF TEXAS HOLD 'EM HANDS

One of the hardest things for beginning Hold 'Em players to understand is the percentage odds assigned to various combinations of hole or pocket cards. In other words, how do you determine which two cards are worth playing and which two cards are worthless?

Obviously, a high pocket pair (jacks, say) will justify a bigger opening bet than a low pocket pair (threes), but how do you calculate the odds of playing less obvious hole cards into advantageous five-card poker hands?

Below is a brief rundown of the most effective opening hands in Texas Hold 'Em, ranked according to *playability*—that is, according to your chances of playing these two cards into a winning five-card poker hand.

The Top 40:

1. A-A
2. K-K
3. Q-Q
4. A-K, suited
5. J-J
6. A-Q, suited
7. A-K
8. 10-10

9. K-Q, suited
10. A-J, suited
11. A-10, suited
12. 9-9
13. A-Q
14. K-J, suited
15. K-Q
16. 8-8
17. K-T, suited
18. A-9, suited
19. A-J
20. Q-J, suited
21. K-J
22. A-8, suited
23. A-10
24. Q-10, suited
25. J-10, suited
26. K-9, suited
27. A-5, suited
28. A-4, suited
29. Q-J
30. A-7, suited
31. K-8, suited
32. K-10
33. Q-9, suited
34. A-3, suited
35. A-6, suited
36. A-2, suited
37. Q-10
38. K-7, suited
39. 7-7
40. J-9, suited

APPENDIX D:
CRIB SHEET 4

THE PROBABILITY OF KEY OPENING HANDS

In Hold 'Em, there are 1,326 possible two-card combinations that can be made from a deck of fifty-two cards. Some of these combinations are always worth playing, while others are pretty much worthless.

Here, courtesy of Bill Burton's *Get the Edge at Low-Limit Texas Hold 'Em*, published by Bonus Books, are the odds of drawing some of the more common opening hands—playable and otherwise.

The probability of holding . . .	Percent	Odds against
Any pair	5.9	16 to 1
Pockets aces, or any specific pair	0.45	220 to 1
Suited cards	23.5	3.25 to 1
Unsuited cards, no pair	70.6	0.4 to 1
All ace-king combinations	1.2	82 to 1
Ace-king, suited	0.3	331 to 1
Ace-ace, king-king, or ace-king	2.1	46 to 1
A single ace	14.9	3.7 to 1
Any "premium hand"—A-A, K-K, Q-Q, A-K, A-Q, K-Q	5	19 to 1

Reprinted by permission

APPENDIX E:
CRIB SHEET 5

A GLOSSARY OF POKER TERMS

Poker players speak a language all their own, and half the time even veteran players have no idea what the guy seated across the table is talking about. First time I heard that someone was sitting next to me with pocket crabs, I thought I should probably move a couple seats farther away from him. (These particular pocket crabs, I later learned, were not communicable—they referred, innocently enough, to a pair of threes, dealt facedown to one of my opponents, so dubbed for the way the numeral 3 can sometimes look like a crab if you stand back and squint after you've had a couple beers.)

Below, in alphabetical order, is a brief description of some of the terms I've used throughout the book, in case I haven't made myself completely clear.

All in—Wagering all of your remaining chips on a single hand

Ante—A small, beginning bet often required of all players participating in a given hand, posted before cards are dealt. In the 2003 World Series of Poker, antes were added in later rounds as a means of increasing the pot action and forcing all players to put at least some of their chips at risk on each hand.

Bad beat—Phrase used to describe a particularly frustrating loss. It usually refers to a big hand losing out on a turn or river card, although in my book all beats are bad beats.

Bet into—As in, "I made a small wager, hoping he would bet into me." This usually refers to a big bet to a player who has previously represented a strong hand.

Blinds—The mandatory bets posted before the start of each new hand, so named because they are made before the cards are seen. The small blind refers to the player seated immediately to the left of the dealer. The big blind refers to the player seated immediately to the left of the small blind. "Stealing blinds" refers to the practice of betting aggressively against a player in the blind positions when there is no other action on a particular hand, in hopes of pushing that player off the pot.

Bluff—To fool, trick, or otherwise deceive an opponent into thinking you have a stronger hand than you actually hold.

Button—The chip-size disk that indicates the dealer position at the table. A player seated "on the button" is last to act in every round of betting following the opening round.

Buy-in—The amount of money required to enter a tournament. The main event at the World Series of Poker carries a $10,000 buy-in, although many players (including yours truly) are allowed to enter the field after winning smaller satellite or promotional tournaments, with much more affordable buy-ins. In my case I entered a $40 online tournament and managed to keep winning until I'd won a World Series seat as a grand prize.

Dead man's hand—Aces and eights, so named because Wild Bill Hickok was said to be holding these two pair when he was shot in the back of the head in a Dakota Territory saloon in 1876.

Draw—To be in a position to make a straight or a flush after the first three community cards have been revealed. An "inside-straight draw," for example, refers to a run of four cards with a break in it, as in a two, three, five, six.

Fifth street—The fifth and final community card in Texas Hold 'Em, also known as "the river."

Fish—A derisive term used to describe a weak player, or an easy target at a particular table.

Flop—The first three community cards in Texas Hold 'Em, dealt together immediately following the first round of betting.

Fourth street—The fourth community card in Texas Hold 'Em, also known as "the turn."

Gut shot—another term for an inside-straight draw. A player holding a 2-3-4-6 before the final community card is hoping to gut-shot (used as a verb) a five on the river.

Heads up—A showdown between two players, after all other players have either folded their hands or been eliminated from a tournament. This is also known as "head-to-head" action.

Hole cards—The two cards dealt facedown to each player at the start of each Hold 'Em hand. They are also known as "pocket" cards. Pocket crabs (threes), pocket rockets (aces), pocket cowboys (kings), and pocket tits (queens—sorry, ladies) are just some variations on the theme.

Kicker—The highest unmatched card alongside a pair, two pairs or three of a kind. If opponents are each holding a pair of twos, for example, the player with the highest kicker will win the hand.

Lay down—To fold a playable hand against a strong bet from an opponent.

Muck—Usually refers to the pile of discarded or previously folded cards in a given hand, but can also be used to describe the act of discarding or folding a hand, as in, "He mucked his cards."

Nuts—The highest possible hand, according to the community cards already on display. After a KD-2D-4D flop, for example, a player holding the ace of diamonds would be said to have the "nut flush draw."

Outs—Usually refers to cards that could potentially turn a losing hand into a winning one or, often, to cards that could potentially complete a powerful hand.

Rags—Low, unsuited, unconnected, and otherwise unwelcome community cards that offer no help in a hand.

Rainbow—Usually refers to a flop representing three different suits, but can also be used to describe all five community cards when all four suits are represented on the board.

River—The fifth and final community card in Texas Hold 'Em, also known as "fifth street."

Scare card—A community card that suggests a strong hand. For example, an ace of hearts on the river can join a previous AD-9H-9C-6S to suggest a powerful full house.

Set—As in, "to flop a set," a pocket pair that combines with a community card to make three of a kind.

Suited—Usually refers to hole cards of the same suit.

Tell—A revealing mannerism, such as a nervous tic, that players try to "read" to gauge the relative strength of an opponent's hand.

Tilt—A state of confusion or uncertainty in which a player might find himself after a couple "bad beats." A player is said to be "on tilt" when he is frustrated or flustered or otherwise off his game.

Turn—The fourth community card in Texas Hold 'Em, also known as "fourth street."

Under the gun—Usually refers to the player seated in the first-to-act position. This can mean the player seated to the immediate left of the big blind in the opening round of betting or the player seated to the immediate left of the dealer in subsequent rounds.